THIS IS OUR FAITH

Series Authors: Janaan Manternach
Carl J. Pfeifer

Authors: Dolores Ready
Joan R. DeMerchant
Maureen Gallagher
Jean Marie Weber

Contributing Author: Kate Sweeney Ristow

SILVER BURDETT GINN
PARSIPPANY, NJ

This Is Our Faith School Program

Contributing Authors: James Bitney, Robert Hamma, Paula A. Lenz, Judene Leon, Yvette Nelson, Sister Carolyn Puccio, C.S.J., Anna Ready, Kate Sweeney Ristow, Barbara Carol Vasiloff, Sister Maureen Shaughnessy, S.C., Sister Cecilia Maureen Cromwell, I.H.M., Patricia Frevert, Mary Lou Ihrig, Sister Arlene Pomije, C.S.J., Sister Mary Agnes Ryan, I.H.M., Brother Michael Sheerin, F.M.S.

Opening Doors: A Take-Home Magazine: Peter H.M. Demkovitz, Janie Gustafson, Margaret Savitskas

Day to Day: Skills for Christian Living: Susan G. Keys

Advisory Board:

Rev. Louis J. Cameli
Philip J. Cunningham
Sister Clare E. Fitzgerald
William J. Freburger
Greer J. Gordon
Sister Veronica R. Grover, S.H.C.J.
Rev. Thomas Guarino
Rev. Robert E. Harahan
Kathleen Hendricks
Rev. Eugene LaVerdieré, S.S.S.
Rev. Frank J. McNulty
Rev. Msgr. John J. Strynkowski

Consultants: Linda Blanchette, Anita Bridge, Fred Brown, Rod Brownfield, Sister Mary Michael Burns, S.C., Pat Burns, Bernadine Carroll, Mary Ellen Cocks, Sister Peggy Conlon, R.S.M., Mary Ann Crowley, Pamela Danni, Sister Jamesetta DeFelice, O.S.U., Sister Mary Elizabeth Duke, S.N.D., Mary M. Gibbons, Yolando Gremillion, Sister Angela Hallahan, C.H.F., Alice T. Heard, Sister Michele O'Connoll, P.B.V.M., Sister Angela O'Mahoney, P.B.V.M., Sister Ruthann O'Mara, S.S.J., Sandra Okulicz-Hulme, Judy Papandria, Rachel Pasano, Sallie Ann Phelan, Sister Geraldine M. Rogers, S.S.J., Mary Lou Schlosser, Patricia Ann Sibilia, Margaret E. Skelly, Lisa Ann Sorlie, Sister Victorine Stoltz, O.S.B., Sister Nancy Jean Turner, S.H.C.J., Christine Ward, Judith Reidel Weber, Kay White, Elizabeth M. Williams, Catherine R. Wolf, Florence Bambrick Yarney, Kathryn K. Zapcic

Nihil Obstat
Kathleen Flanagan, S.C., Ph.D.
Censor Librorum
Ellen Joyce, S.C. Ph.D.
Censor Librorum

Imprimatur
✠ Most Reverend Frank J. Rodimer
Bishop of Paterson

November 8, 1996

The *nihil obstat* and *imprimatur* are official declarations that a book or pamphlet is free of doctrinal and moral error. No implication is contained therein that those who have granted the *nihil obstat* and *imprimatur* agree with the contents, opinions, or statements expressed.

Acknowledgments

Scripture selections are taken from *The New American Bible* © 1986, 1970 Confraternity of Christian Doctrine, Washington, DC. Used with permission.

Scripture texts used in this work are taken from *The New American Bible with Revised New Testament* ©1986 by the Confraternity of Christian Doctrine, Washington, D.C., and are used with permission of copyright owner. All rights reserved.

Excerpts from the English translation of *The Roman Missal* © 1973, International Committee on English in the Liturgy, Inc. (ICEL); excerpts from the English translation of *The Rite of Baptism for Children* © 1969, International Committee on English in the Liturgy, Inc. (ICEL); excerpts from the English translation of *Book of Blessings* © 1988, ICEL.
All rights reserved.

ISBN 0-382-304942

1 2 3 4 5 6 7 8 9 10–W–05 04 03 02 01 00 99 98 97

Contents

LET US
PRAY

Let Us Pray

Sign of the Cross

In the Name of the Father,
and of the Son,
and of the Holy Spirit.
Amen.

The Lord's Prayer

Our Father, who art in heaven,
hallowed be thy name;
thy kingdom come;
thy will be done on earth
as it is in heaven.
Give us this day our daily bread;
and forgive us our trespasses
as we forgive those
who trespass against us;
and lead us not into temptation,
but deliver us from evil.
Amen.

Let Us Pray

Hail Mary

Hail Mary, full of grace,
the Lord is with you.
Blessed are you among women,
and blessed is the fruit
of your womb, Jesus.
Holy Mary, Mother of God,
pray for us sinners, now,
and at the hour of our death.
Amen.

Glory Be to the Father

Glory be to the Father,
and to the Son,
and to the Holy Spirit.
As it was in the beginning,
is now, and ever shall be,
world without end.
Amen.

Grace Before Meals

Bless us, O Lord,
and these your gifts,
which we are about to receive
from your goodness,
through Christ our Lord.
Amen.

Grace After Meals

We give you thanks
for all your gifts,
almighty God,
living and reigning
now and forever.
Amen.

Let Us Pray

A Morning Prayer

My God, I offer you today
all I think and do and say,
uniting it with what was
done on earth,
by Jesus Christ,
your Son.
Amen.

Evening Prayer

Dear God, before I sleep
I want to thank you
for this day so full
of your kindness and
your joy.
I close my eyes to rest
safe in your loving care.
Amen.

Beginning the Journey

We are on our way to learn more about God.
What do you already know about God?

Here is a picture of me.

This is my teacher's name.

Here is my family.

We are on a journey together to learn more about God.

Prayer for the Journey

Leader This is the Bible, the book of God's word.
Let us listen to Jesus' promise to be with us on our journey.
Wherever we are, he is with us.
Here are his words.
"Behold, I am with you always" (Matthew 28:20).

The word of the Lord!

All Thanks be to God.

Leader May God bless each of us as we begin our journey.
May he bless these books, which we will use as our map along the way.

All Amen!

A Profile of the First-Grade Child

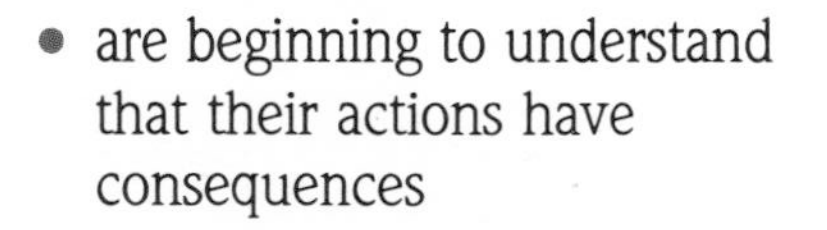

No one knows your first grader better than you! It may be helpful and interesting to you as a parent or guardian, however, to explore some of the characteristics of the first grader.

First graders

- learn that they are unique and lovable through your words and actions
- depend upon their families to care for their needs
- have a natural curiosity
- are self-centered and may have difficulty sharing
- have short emotional fuses
- have short attention spans
- need concrete experiences
- are responsive to religious practices that convey a sense of mystery
- are beginning to understand that their actions have consequences
- can begin to express their own simple prayers
- have experienced being hurt and have experienced forgiveness

Take Time You may want to make a special effort this week to notice the unique personality and giftedness of your first grader. Be sure to affirm him or her often. Cherish the great gift your child is to you and your family!

to continue in faith the same journey you first embarked on when you presented your son or daughter for Baptism. Throughout the years you have been—and continue to be—the most important person of faith for your child. As your first-grader commits to this year's faith journey, you are invited as the primary educator in faith to journey along with your child, in whatever way is most comfortable for you. THIS IS OUR FAITH is privileged to assist you in this important task.

This Year In Grade 1

This year your first grader will be introduced to some of the basic teachings that the Catholic Church teaches about the Blessed Trinity. He or she will discover much about God the Father, Son, and Holy Spirit.

The first unit introduces God as creator. Your child will also be presented with a picture of God as a loving parent. God blesses us with a multitude of gifts. In order to recognize something of the goodness and blessings that fill God's creation, your child will consider all the wonderful gifts God has given him or her. Chief among these gifts will be Jesus, God's most special gift to us.

As your child completes each unit of THIS IS OUR FAITH, you will receive a take-home magazine entitled *Opening Doors: A Take-Home Magazine*. Each magazine will include the following features to help you grow in your faith and to help you share that faith with your child.

A Closer Look

includes an article relating the unit theme to a particular aspect of the Mass and family interactive pages for you and your child to enjoy together.

Being Catholic

highlights a particular aspect of our Catholic heritage.

Growing Closer

suggests activities to help you and your family integrate your faith into everyday life.

And also . . .

Looking Ahead

previews the next unit of THIS IS OUR FAITH.

Our Father

Our Father,
who art in heaven,
hallowed be thy name;
thy kingdom come;
thy will be done
on earth as it is in heaven.

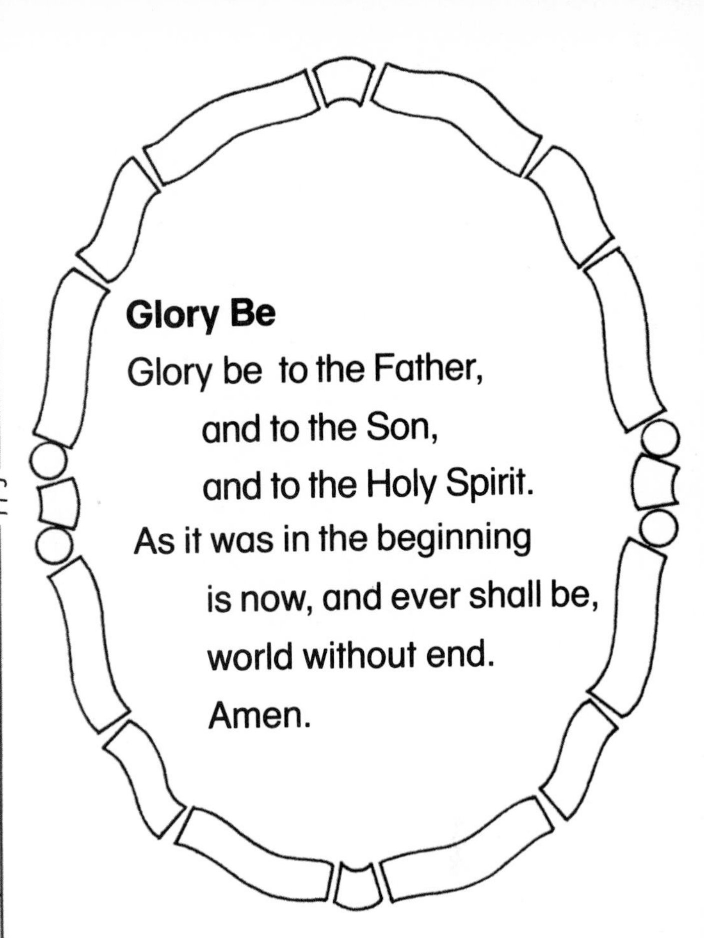

Glory Be

Glory be to the Father,
and to the Son,
and to the Holy Spirit.
As it was in the beginning
is now, and ever shall be,
world without end.
Amen.

Dear Parents,
Assist your child in making this booklet.
During the year, help your child to learn the prayers.

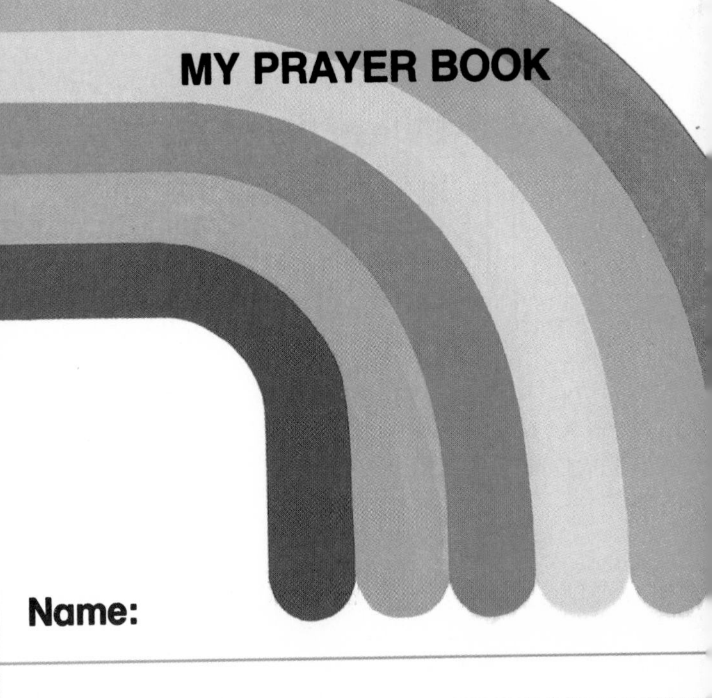

MY PRAYER BOOK

Name:

Hail Mary

Hail Mary, full of grace!
The Lord is with you.
Blessed are you
among women,
and blessed is the fruit
of your womb, Jesus.

Holy Mary, Mother of God,
pray for us sinners
now and at the hour
of our death.
Amen.

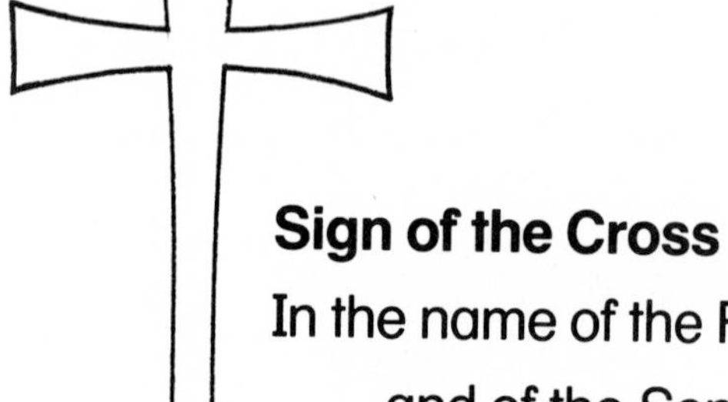

Sign of the Cross

In the name of the Father,
and of the Son,
and of the Holy Spirit.
Amen.

Give us this day
our daily bread;
and forgive us our trespasses
as we forgive those
who trespass against us;
and lead us not
into temptation,
but deliver us from evil.
Amen.

UNIT 1

God Gives Us Many Gifts

What kinds of gifts do you like to receive?

1

God Makes Us Special

Everyone is special. Name two things that make you special.

I Am Special

My face is my own
And so is my name.
I am like many others,
But not just the same.

I am glad that I am.
I am happy to be
Like so many others,
Yet special, that's ME!

Activity

1. Show how you are special.
   Put your fingerprints here.

2. Circle three things you can do. Tell about them.

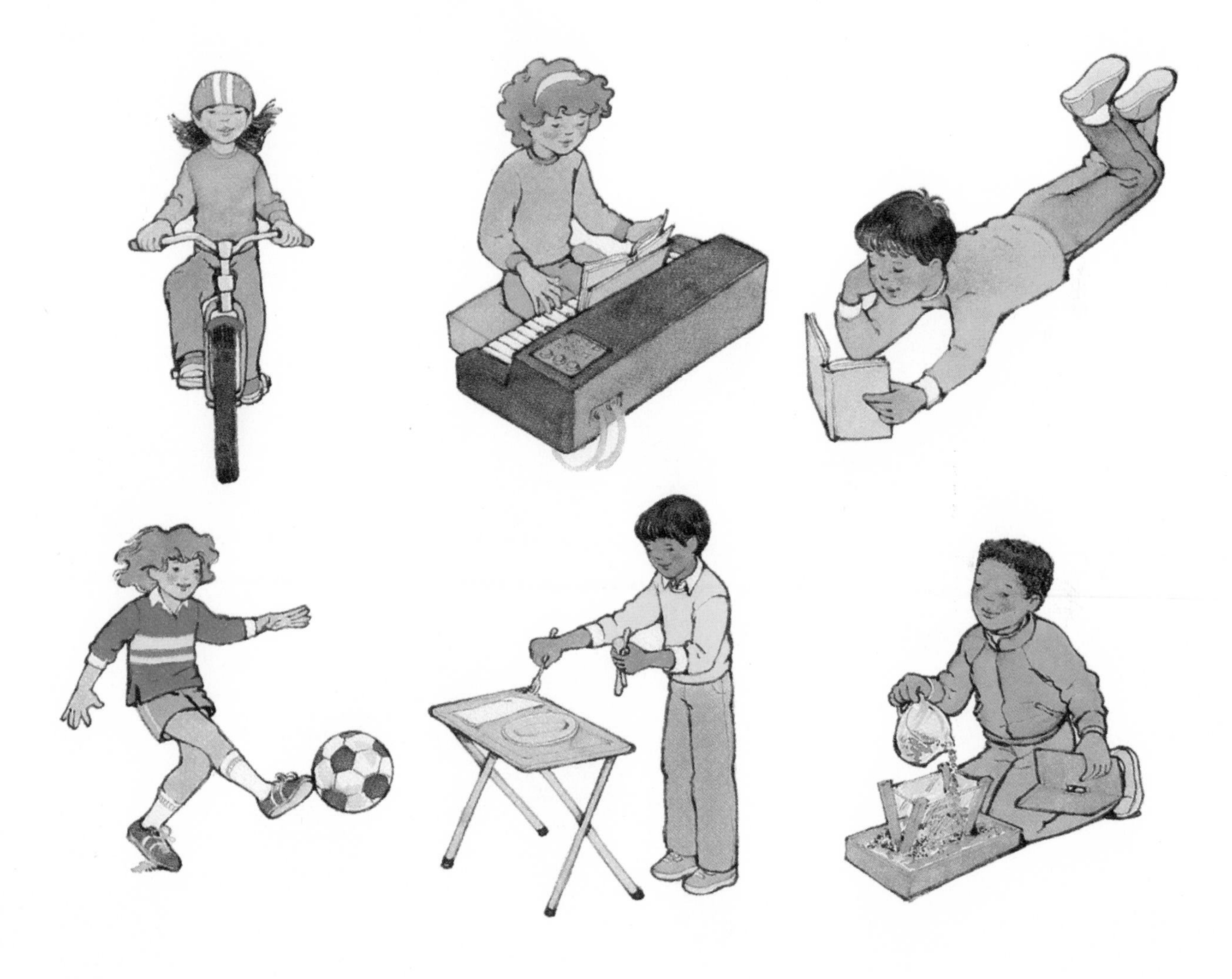

God Knows Us

God tells us that we are special.

God says, "You are precious and I love you."

Based on Isaiah 43:4

Our Special Book

The **Bible** is a special book about God's love for us.
In the Bible, God says,
"I made you because I love you."
God's love makes each of us special.

Based on Wisdom 11:24

Thank You, God

God made me very special,
And so I smile and say,
"O God, I want to thank you
For making me this way."

Activity

It is good to thank God for making us so special.
Trace the letters to complete the prayer. Then pray it.

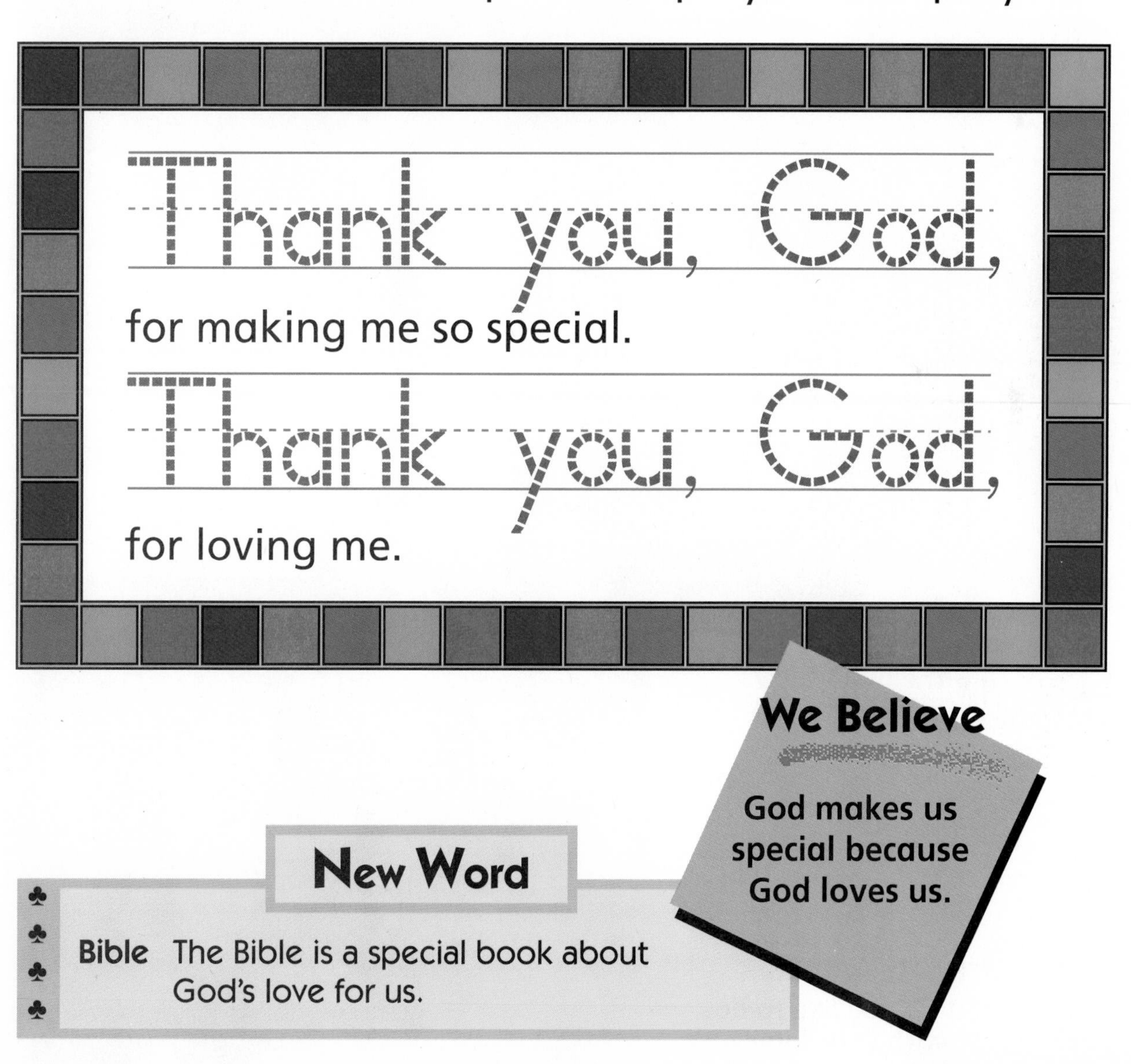

We Believe

God makes us special because God loves us.

New Word

Bible The Bible is a special book about God's love for us.

God Loves Our Family

The Bible tells us that God made everyone. So all of us are the children of God. God loves each of us. And God loves each of our families. Each of our families is very special.

▼ What do children like to do with their grandparents?

▲ How are the people in your family special?

What do you like to do with your family? ▶

Enjoy this poem with your teacher.

Berta and her family
Like to juggle balls.
Timmy and his family
Like to see waterfalls.

Miki and her family
Like to take long hikes.
Jacy and his family
Like to ride red bikes.

Families are special
In all that they do.
Families are special.
Your family is too.

Activity

Color each object that the families are using as they do special things together.

What are some things you do with your family?

Being Special, Acting Special

God made us all special,
so we can act in special ways.
We can love others.
We can help our family and friends.
When we show love to others,
we act like God.
That is very special!

▲ How do you help others?

▲ How do you help other people feel happy?

▼ How do you show that you are special?

Activity

Look at the pictures.

Tell how these people are helping.

Circle one special way you will help.

Praying By Bowing

All: Thank you, God, for the Bible, our special book about your love for us. Amen.

Chapter Review

God makes each of us special. Color the pictures to show what is special about each child.

1. Who makes you so special? ______
2. What is the name of the special book about God's love for us? ______
3. Tell what is special about you.

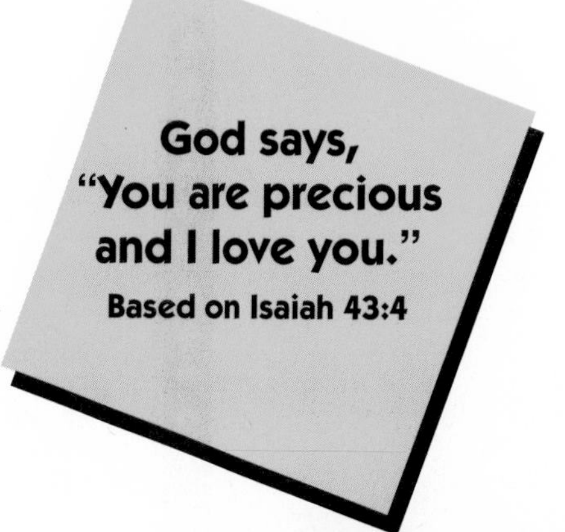

God Gives Us Special Gifts

God Created a Wonderful World

God made the  and the .

God covered the empty land with 

and  .

God filled the seas with  .

God sent  up into the sky.

All over the land, God put animals,

 and  .

What are some things in God's world that you like?

God saw how very good everything was.

God loved it all. Then God made  .

God gave them the  full of special 

Based on Genesis 1:1–31

God's Gift of the World

God wanted to **create** the world for us.
God made the whole world out of nothing.
God loves the world and all the people in it.
God loves the animals, the plants,
and all the things in it.
The world is a special gift from God to us.

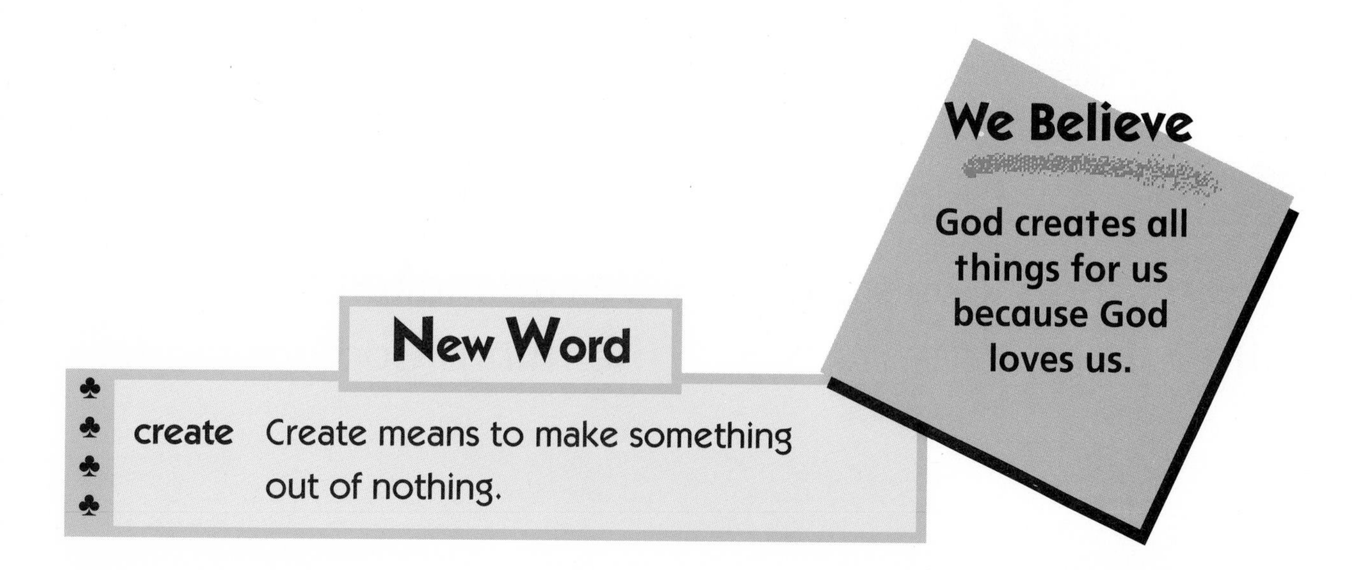

We Believe

God creates all things for us because God loves us.

New Word

create Create means to make something out of nothing.

God's Wonderful World

We can enjoy God's world.

We can care for all that God has made.

We can share God's gifts with others.

We can make things from the things God has made.

God's Wonderful Colors

God uses many colors to create our wonderful world.
Which color is your favorite?

Activity

What would our world look like if God had used only one color to create the world?
Let's find out! Color everything in the first box with only your favorite color.
Then color the next box with many of the colors God made.

Which picture do you like best?
Why do you think God used many colors to create our wonderful world?

Caring for God's Wonderful World

God made our wonderful world.

God made people, animals, plants, and things.

We can care for God's world and everything in it.

Activity

Finish each of the five picture stories.

Draw what you think will happen next in each story.

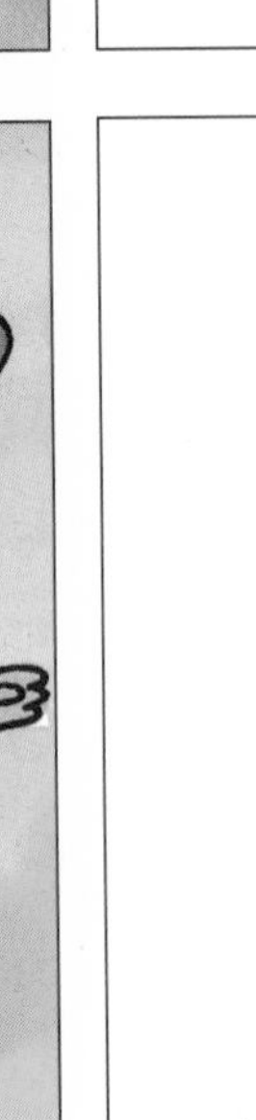

Tell a story about how you care for God's world.

Using God's Wonderful World

God made many wonderful things.
We can use them to make other things.
People use wheat to make bread
and wood to make houses.
People can use cotton to make cloth.
Here is the story of cotton.

From Cotton to Clothes

God gives us cotton plants.

Farmers pick the cotton with big machines.

The cotton is spun into yarn at the factory.

An artist draws colored flowers for the new cloth.

A woman weaves the pattern into the cloth.

Workers sew the cloth into clothes for us.

At the store, a salesperson hangs up the new clothes.

We shop at the store and try on the new clothes.

Our Prayer Today

Thank you, God, for letting people help to make nice things.

Praying in Our Own Words

We can make up our own prayers.
We can make up a prayer to thank God.

Activity

Draw a picture of something you want to thank God for.

Thank You, God

Look at your picture.
Pray the prayer you made up.
The other children can help you.
They can pray, "Thank you, God."

Chapter Review

We can use the things God created.

God makes peanuts.

We can make other things from peanuts.

Put the pictures in order.

Write **1**, **2**, **3**, and **4** in the correct box.

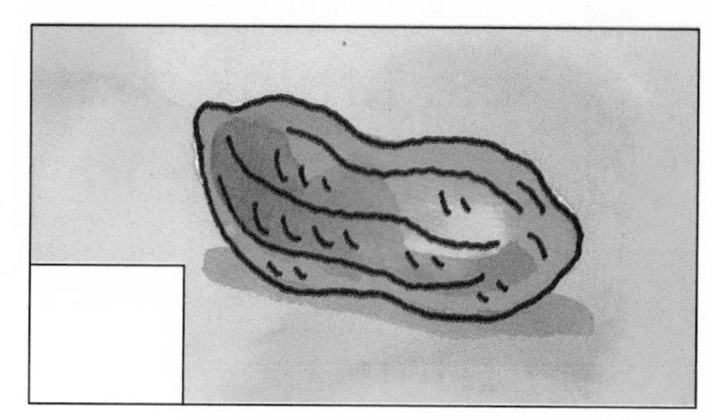

1. Who made the world?

2. What word means to make something out of nothing?

3. Talk about what you can thank God for.

Give thanks to God because God is good.
Based on Psalm 13

3

God Gives Us Special People

Special people love us and we love them, too. Who are some special people in your life?

Special People in My Life

Aunt people, uncle people,
Parent people, too.
Teacher people, friend people,
Grandparents who
Are with me when I need them,
Are for me when I cry.
All these people love me,
And I think that I know why.
It's just because I'm special!
And so are they, you see.
I could not be without them.
We are a family.

God Cares for Us

God gives us people to love us and help us.
God takes care of us through these people.

We Believe

God gives us special people to love and care for us.

Activity

Look at the pictures on both pages.
Choose a picture that reminds you
of someone who loves you.
Tell a story about that special person.

God Gives Us People

God scooped up some clay.
God formed a man from the clay of the earth.

God gave him a garden full of flowers and fruit.
The man liked them all, but he felt very lonely.

So God made dogs and cats, tigers and giraffes, birds and butterflies for the man.
He liked them all, but still the man felt lonely.

"The man needs a friend," God thought.
So God made a woman to be with the man.

"At last," the man said, "God
has created a woman so I am no
longer alone.
Her mind and heart are like mine.
We can love each other and share
God's gifts."

Based on Genesis 2:4–24

God Knows We Need People

God, our loving **Creator**, gives us special people to love and care for us.
These people are gifts from God to us.

New Word

Creator Our Creator is God, who makes everything in the world out of nothing.

God's Law of Love

God creates us to be friends.
We can be friends with God, our Creator.
We can be friends with each other.
We can be friends with ourselves, too.

We can love God.
We can love others.
We can love ourselves.
When we love, we do good things.
When we love, we do unselfish things.

Activity

Try to get to the people walking in space.

1. You will need a coin and a button.
2. Flip the coin to see how many spaces to move the button.

   Heads = 1 space

   Tails = 2 spaces

We Can Choose to Be Unselfish

Everything God created is good.
Each of us is good.
But sometimes we can be selfish.
Sometimes we choose not to do
good things for others.
We do not have to be selfish.
We can choose to be unselfish
and to love others.

Activity

Circle the pictures of children choosing to love.

Choose to Love

Ann sets a butterfly free.
Sam won't share his apple tree.
Flo won't share her ball or truck.
Gan lets others pet his duck.
Carl has to win each game.
Lani treats us all the same.

Draw a circle around the pictures of the children who are choosing not to show love.
Then tell how they can become loving and unselfish.

Praying a Prayer of Thanks

In the hearts, draw pictures of the special people you want to thank God for.

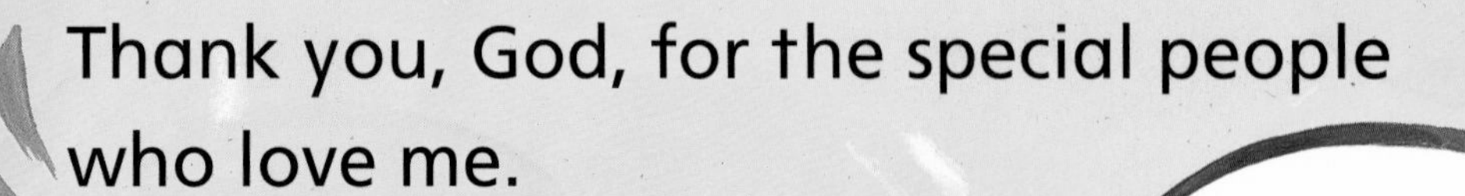

Thank you, God, for the special people who love me.

Thank you, God, for . . .

Thank you, God, for . . .

Thank you, God, for . . .

Thank you, God, for loving me.
Amen.

Chapter Review

God wants us to show love for others.
The picture shows children being selfish.
In the heart below, draw them
being unselfish.

1. Who is our Creator? ______________

2. Who gives us special people?

____

3. Talk about what you can do for the people you love.

God says,
"People need other people."
Based on
Genesis 2:18

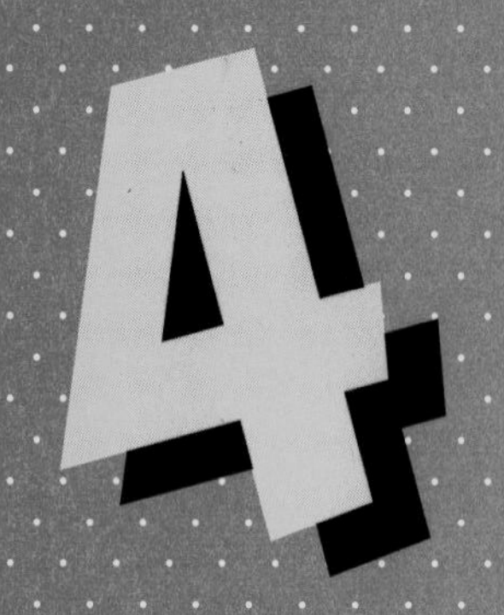

God Gives Us Jesus

God's Best Gift

What do you think is the best gift God gives us?

God loved all  .

But some  forgot about God.

They forgot God loved all

and promised to be with them always.

The  came for God to help

them remember.

God chose to give 

the best  of all.

What do you think is the best gift God gives us?

God's best gift to us is

Jesus .

Activity

Color the part of the picture that shows the best gift God has ever given to us.

Jesus Is Our Friend

God gives us **Jesus** to be our friend.
Jesus is the Son of God.
Jesus, our friend, loves us very much.
This story from the Bible shows how
much Jesus loves children.

Jesus and the Children

One day Jesus felt tired.
He wanted to sit down and rest.
But some mothers, fathers, and
children came to meet Jesus.
Some friends of Jesus
told the people to go away.
"Leave Jesus alone," they said.
"He is tired."
But Jesus said, "I am never
too tired to talk to children.
Let them come to me!
I love them very much."

Then Jesus hugged the children.
He held them on his lap and
blessed them.
Jesus and the children were happy.
They were friends.

Based on Mark 10:13–16

We Believe

Jesus is God's most special gift to us. Jesus is the Son of God.

New Word

Jesus Jesus is the Son of God and our friend.

Jesus and the Bible

In the Bible, there are stories that
Jesus told about God, his Father.
Jesus told the story below.
Listen to it to hear about the great
love a father has for his son.
It is like God's great love for us.

A Father Loves His Son

One day, a son left home
and got into trouble.
Then the son remembered his
father's love and came home.
His father was so happy!
He gave a party for his son.
The father said, "Let us celebrate!
My son has come home."

Based on Luke 15:11–32

Besides stories about his Father's love,
there are stories about Jesus' love
in the Bible.
Here is one.

A Crippled Woman

One day Jesus saw a woman
who was bent over.
She could not stand up straight.
Jesus said to her,
"You are healed."
Jesus touched her and
she stood up straight.

How happy she was that
Jesus loved and cared for her.
Now she knew what God is like.
God is full of love for us.

Based on Luke 13:10–13

Needing to "Be Saved"

Activity

Tell what kind of help each child above needs. How could you help save each child?

Jesus Saves Us

The Bible says that Jesus saves us.
How does he save us?
Jesus helps us remember that God loves us and that we are very special.

We call Jesus our **Savior** because he saves us when we forget God's love.

Jesus says, "I am always with you."
So we can always ask Jesus to save us.
We can always say, "Save me, Jesus!
Help me remember that God loves me."

New Word

Savior Our Savior is Jesus, the Son of God and our friend. He saves us and helps us.

Praying the Sign of the Cross

Friends of Jesus pray a prayer called The Sign of the Cross.
It helps us remember that God loves us.
This special prayer helps us remember that Jesus is God's best gift to us.

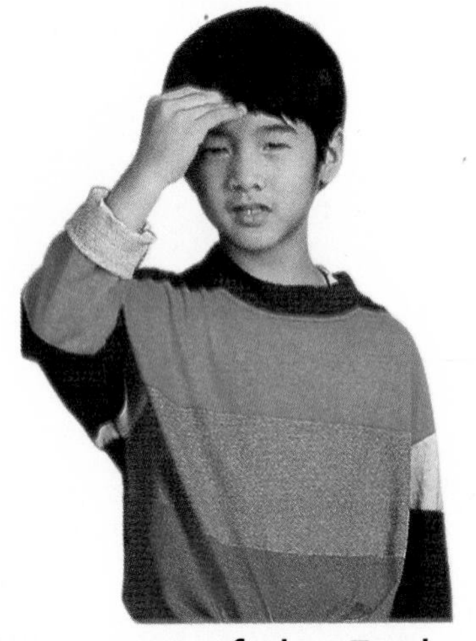

In the name of the Father,

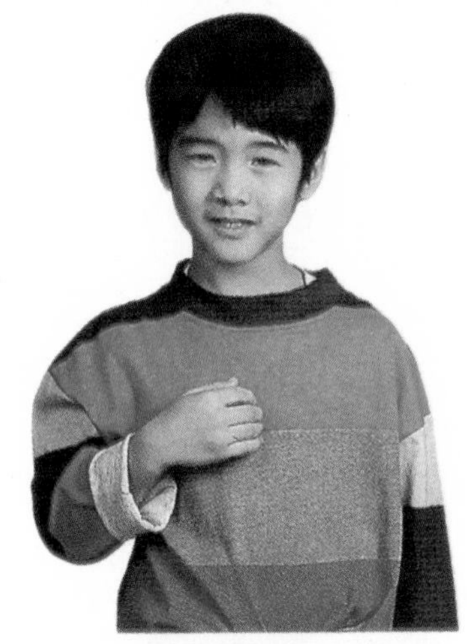

and of the Son,

and of the Holy Spirit.

Amen.

Chapter Review

Cross out all the **B** letters to find a message.

B	B	J	E	S	U	S	B	B	I	S	B	M	Y	B	B	F	R	I	E	N	D	B	B

Copy the message below.

1. Who is God's Son and our friend?

2. What does Jesus, our Savior, help us to remember?

3. Tell what you know and like about Jesus.

Jesus says, "I am always with you."
Matthew 28:20

Unit 1 Organizer

Draw
God's Gifts to Us

ME

THE WORLD

MY FAMILY

JESUS

MY FRIENDS

Unit 1 Review

Look at the words in the box.
Choose a word to finish each sentence.
Write the word below the sentence.

loves	God	thank	share

1. ______ created you to be special.

2. God made us because God ______ us.

3. We say ______ you for God's gifts.

4. We can ______ God's gifts with others.

Unit 1 Review

Draw a line to the word that ends each sentence.

1. Our Creator is _________• • Jesus

2. The special book about God's love is the ________• • God

3. God's most special gift is __• • Bible

Circle the correct answer.

1. Each person is special and God loves us all.

   Yes No

2. Jesus is never with us.

   Yes No

3. Jesus is our Savior.

   Yes No

4. Jesus is God's brother.

   Yes No

5. "Create" means to make something out of nothing.

   Yes No

6. God gives us special people to love and care for us.

   Yes No

FEELINGS, GIFTS FROM GOD

Boots and Zip are
good friends.
They are happy
to see each other.

"Boots, let's play ball when
we get home," Zip said.
"Oh, not today.
I get to help my dad wash
the car," Boots said proudly.
Zip was disappointed.

In this story, each person has many different feelings.
Boots and Zip both feel happy to see each other.
Boots feels proud, but Zip feels disappointed.

Activity

Circle one of the words below.

Draw a picture of a time you felt like the word you circled.

Happy **Proud** **Disappointed**

Following Jesus

Our feelings are a gift from God.

Each of us has many different feelings.

Our feelings are a part of what makes us special.

Growing Closer

BEDTIME offers family members an opportunity to spend a few quiet moments together. A good way to share your love with your children at this time is to call down God's blessing on each of them. Touch your child's head while simply saying, "God bless you," or use your own words. Allow your child to bless you, too!

ALL OF US have been gifted by a gracious and generous God. Set this week aside as "Gratitude Week" in your family. Make a family list of all of the gifts, blessings, and talents your family has enjoyed. Use this list as part of your family meal prayer or bedtime prayer. Be sure to make a special effort to thank one another, too!

Looking Ahead

Unit 2 will focus on Jesus, the Son of God, who came to live among us. By appreciating Jesus, your child can begin to know him as a friend. As your child grows older, he or she will come to recognize Jesus as a leader whose unparalleled courage, sensitivity, and compassion to others bear witness to who Jesus is.

OPENING DOORS

A Take-Home Magazine™

Thank You!

We live in a time when we supposedly never "get something for nothing." When we find ourselves echoing this jaded attitude, it is time to remember that generosity still exists. God's generosity toward us never diminishes.

Catholics have a way of expressing their gratitude to God by celebrating the Eucharist, or Mass. The word *eucharist* means "thanksgiving" and the Mass is our prayer of thanksgiving.

During the Liturgy of the Word, we hear the good news that God loves us. Each Sunday, we listen to stories of divine interaction in the individual lives and in the community life of God's people, and we know that God is equally concerned for us today. God's generosity is unbounded. To this graciousness we respond,

"Thanks be to God."

At the beginning of the eucharistic prayer, we pray,

"It is right to give him thanks and praise."

Grazie

Arigato

Thank you

Gracias

hands in prayer carries a strong message—I am united with a group of people who repeatedly thank God for their blessings. I understand that this is important because we do it over and over. Both repetition and community are essential to ritual, a corporate symbolic action that we do over and over again.

Another way of praying can be introduced gently to children — that of meditating. Children love stories, especially those that touch the heart, and none do this better than the stories of Jesus. The scripture accounts not only relate events in the life of Jesus but also develop a relationship with him. After reading a biblical selection, help your child produce standup cutouts of the characters. Keep the cutouts in a place accessible to the children. During play, they will recall the details of the story and relive the emotions. In this way their imaginations and hearts are engaged with the person of Jesus — a kind of mental prayer.

Sources of help for family prayer are listed below:

Catholic Household Blessings and Prayers published by The United States Catholic Conference offers table prayers, bedside prayers, blessings, and simple rituals.

This Is Our Faith Family Prayer Book published by Silver Burdett and Ginn contains traditional Church prayers in addition to a wide variety of prayers for everyday use in family life.

Being Catholic

Family Prayer

> "Prayer begins very early in childhood by hearing others pray; even small children can learn to call upon the Father, Jesus, and the Holy Spirit. In time, the child will become familiar with the various prayers . . . and make them part of his or her life" (Sharing the Light of Faith: National Catechetical Directory for Catholics of the United States #145).

Many families find mealtimes convenient to introduce different types of prayer. Young children respond well to simple rituals such as holding hands during grace. This may seem like a very simple thing to do, but when you think about it, this ceremony has much significance.

What exactly is a ritual? It is an action that conveys meaning. The fact that it is practiced by a group of people makes it even more meaningful. Take for example the childhood ritual, superstitious though it is, of avoiding cracks in sidewalks. This is not a mere game; it conveys the conventional wisdom of the group that stepping on a crack will "break your mother's back." So, too, the joining of

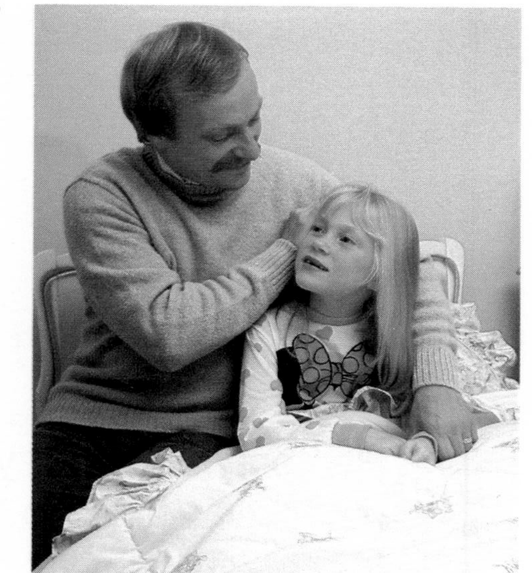

Obrigado Thank You

During the eucharistic prayer, fleeting thoughts cross our minds as we thank God for all of creation. We express our gratitude for our own humanity; for the diversity of nature: "male and female he created them" (Genesis 1:27), of every race and color; for varieties of landscapes, climate, and cultures. We acknowledge God as the source of all goodness.

As we pray the eucharistic prayer, we do not pray alone. Re-enacting the Lord's supper, we know that Jesus is with us, and we unite our prayers with his. Praising Jesus for his passion, death, and resurrection, we thank God for our salvation. No more fitting prayer of thanksgiving could be offered.

As we are dismissed to love and serve the Lord, we respond,
"Thanks be to God."

Leaving the church, we are thankful that God goes with us as we work with Jesus to continue the building of the kingdom.

Thank You!

Your child knows the joy of both giving and receiving gifts. Use this understanding to introduce these concepts as they relate to the Mass. Reading the rebus story below with your child will help you identify some of the gifts for which we thank God and the gifts we offer.

At  I say, "Thank You," for

the gifts God has given me. I give

 to God, too.

I offer God gifts of  and  .

I offer God the gift of myself. God is very

 with my gifts!  gives

himself to us as the Bread of Life. Jesus is

God's best  !

Remember to offer your gifts to God the next time you go to Mass. Thank God for the gifts that have been given you.

UNIT 2

Jesus Learned About Life

From whom do you learn most?

5

Jesus Grew Up in a Family

Who are the people you belong with?

A family is a group of people who belong together.

Families Are Special

A family is people
Like you and like me,
Who are all together
On one family tree.

A family is people
Who need one another,
The young and the old,
The sister and brother.

A family is people
Who always are there
For working and playing,
For kindness and care.

The Family of Jesus

Jesus, God's own Son, grew up in a family, just as we do. He lived with Mary and Joseph. Jesus' family is the **Holy Family.**

New Word

Holy Family Mary, Joseph, and Jesus are the Holy Family.

We Believe

Jesus is the Son of God and human, too. We call Jesus and his family the Holy Family.

The Holy Family

The Holy Family lived in **Nazareth.**
Most people there lived in houses
made from stone and mud.
The Holy Family probably did, too.

In their house, Joseph had a workplace.
He was a carpenter.
With his hammer and nails, he could
build chests and stools.
With his saw and ax, Joseph cut wood.

Mary and Joseph cared for Jesus
and for each other.
She and Joseph taught Jesus that
members of a family love each other.

Jesus loved his family.
They cried together in sad times.
They laughed together in happy times.
They thanked God for each other.

New Word

Nazareth Nazareth is the town where Jesus lived with Mary and Joseph.

Activity

In the space below, draw the faces of the people in your family.
Write their names under their pictures.

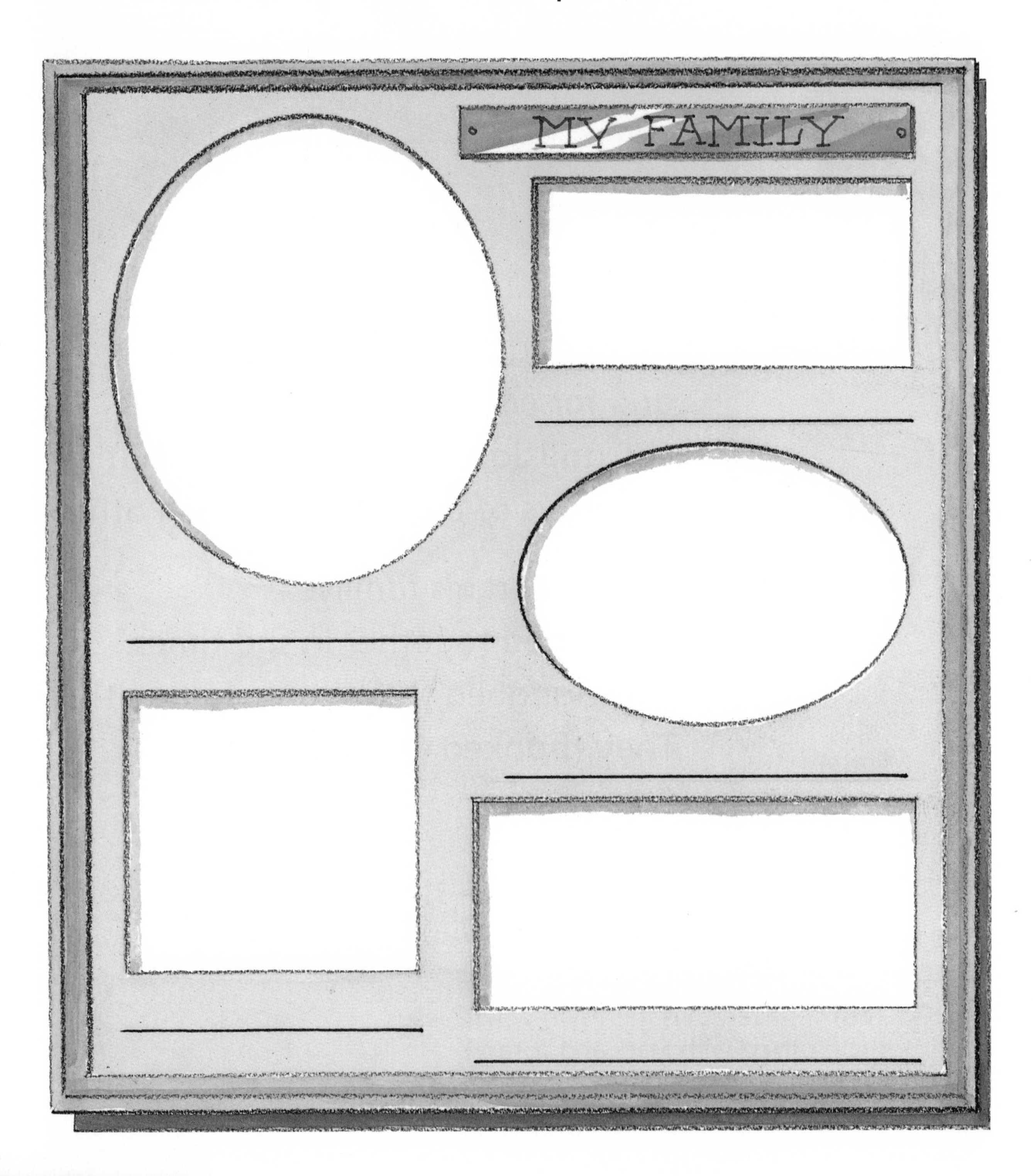

Jesus' Family

Jesus was part of a family.
He had relatives named Zechariah,
Elizabeth, and their son, John.
Zechariah led the people in prayer.
He helped them to remember God's love.

Jesus' family did many things to remember God's love. Even their names reminded them that God was always with them.

Mary
The very best

Elizabeth
God makes me happy.

Jesus
God saves and helps us.

John
God has blessed me.

Joseph
God gives more than I can even think of asking for.

Zechariah
God is always thinking of me and helping me.

The Holy Family Helps and Cares

Mary and Joseph brought up Jesus to be a caring person.

Joseph and Jesus often walked together to evening prayer. On the way, they might have talked over their day. Maybe, they chatted about what Jesus and Joseph built. They might even have thought of ways to surprise Mary.

The Holy Family loved and cared for each other. They showed their love by helping one another.

Activity

What surprise might Joseph and Jesus have planned for Mary?

We Help Our Families

Jesus helped Mary and Joseph.
God wants us to be like Jesus.
God wants us to help our families, too.

Activity

Draw lines to match the pictures that show family members helping one another and showing love.

Praying with the Psalms

When Jesus was growing up,
he learned some prayers in the Bible.
These prayers are called psalms.
We can pray this psalm with Jesus
and his Holy Family.

How wonderful it is,
and how pleasant,
for the family of God
to live together
in peace and love.

Based on Psalm 133:1

Chapter Review

Jesus, Mary, and Joseph cared for one another. Draw a line between the things each member of the Holy Family used to help the others.

1. Name the people in Jesus' family.

2. Where did Jesus grow up?

3. Talk about how Jesus is like us.

Children, love and help your parents. Parents, be good to your children.
Based on Ephesians 6:1,4

6

Mary, the Mother of Jesus

Suzy and Her Mother

Look at the pictures of this mother with her child, Suzy.
What are three things the mother does that make her special to Suzy?

What are some things that you think make a mother special?

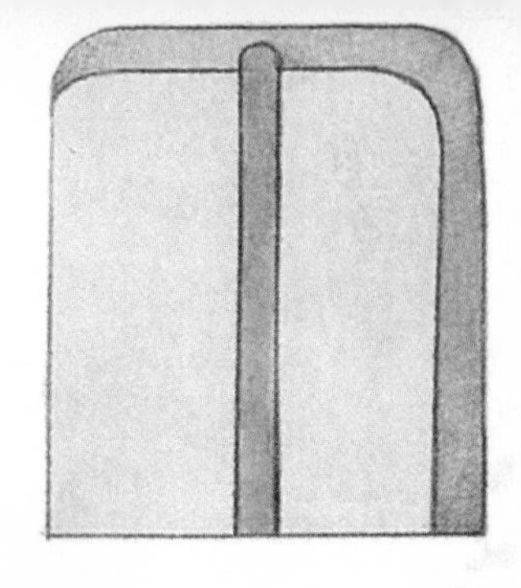

A Message for Mary

One day, God sent an angel to give
a message to Mary.
She was a young woman who
lived in Nazareth.
The angel's name was Gabriel.

"Hail Mary," the angel said.
"God wants you to be the mother
of a special baby boy.
You will name the baby Jesus.
He will be called the Son of God."

Mary loved God,
so she said to Gabriel,
"Yes, I will be the mother of Jesus.
I will do what God asks of me."

Then the angel left Mary.
She prayed about the baby
who was coming.

Based on Luke 1:26–38

New Word

angel An angel is a messenger and helper from God.

Mary Is Our Mother, Too

When God asked Mary to be
Jesus' mother, she said, "Yes!"
She remembered that God loved her.
Mary trusted God's love.

As Jesus grew up, he saw how much
Mary trusted God.
Mary also showed Jesus how to love others.
She helped him remember God's love.

Because Jesus loves us, he shares his
mother with us.
Our Mother Mary loves us and wants us
to be happy.

Mary Loves Us

- Mary taught Jesus to be kind.
  She can teach us to be like Jesus.

- Mary likes to hear our stories.
  She knows about being happy,
  and she knows about being sad.

- Mary is a mother to us.
  She wants to hear our troubles.
  Mary will ask God to help us.

Activity

Trace the letters. Then complete the prayer.

We Believe

Mary is the mother of Jesus, God's Son. Mary is our Mother, too.

Our Lady of Guadalupe

Mary Loves All People

Jesus loves all the people in the world. Mary loves them, too.

People make beautiful pictures and statues of her. Statues can help us remember that Mary loves us. Which picture or statue do you like best?

Korean, "Virgin and Child"

Our Lady of Fatima

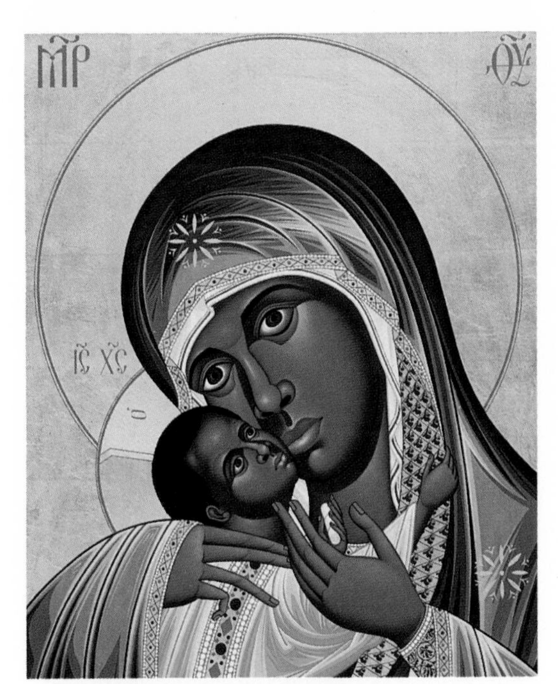

"Mother of the Streets" by Robert Lentz.
Courtesy of Bridge Building Images, Inc.

"Cheyenne Virgin and Child" by Father John Giuliani.
Courtesy of Bridge Building Images, Inc.

Activity

Show your love for Mary with a drawing. In the space below, draw a picture of Mary.

Courtesy of S.M.A. Fathers

Remembering Mary's Love

When someone loves us, we often remember special things that they do and say.

We remember that the angel
Gabriel visited Mary in Nazareth.
Mary said yes to God's messenger.

We remember that Mary rode
a donkey all the way to Bethlehem.
She gave birth to Jesus.

We remember that Mary loves Jesus
and that she loves us, too.

We Honor Mary

To show that we love Mary, we do special things.

▲ We name churches after Mary.

▲ We pray the Rosary and think of Mary and her son, Jesus.

▲ We walk and sing songs about Mary.

Activity

Circle the way you would like to honor Mary.

Praying The Hail Mary

We can say a special prayer.
In this prayer, we remember
one of Mary's stories.
We remember that the angel Gabriel
came from God to ask Mary to be Jesus' mother.

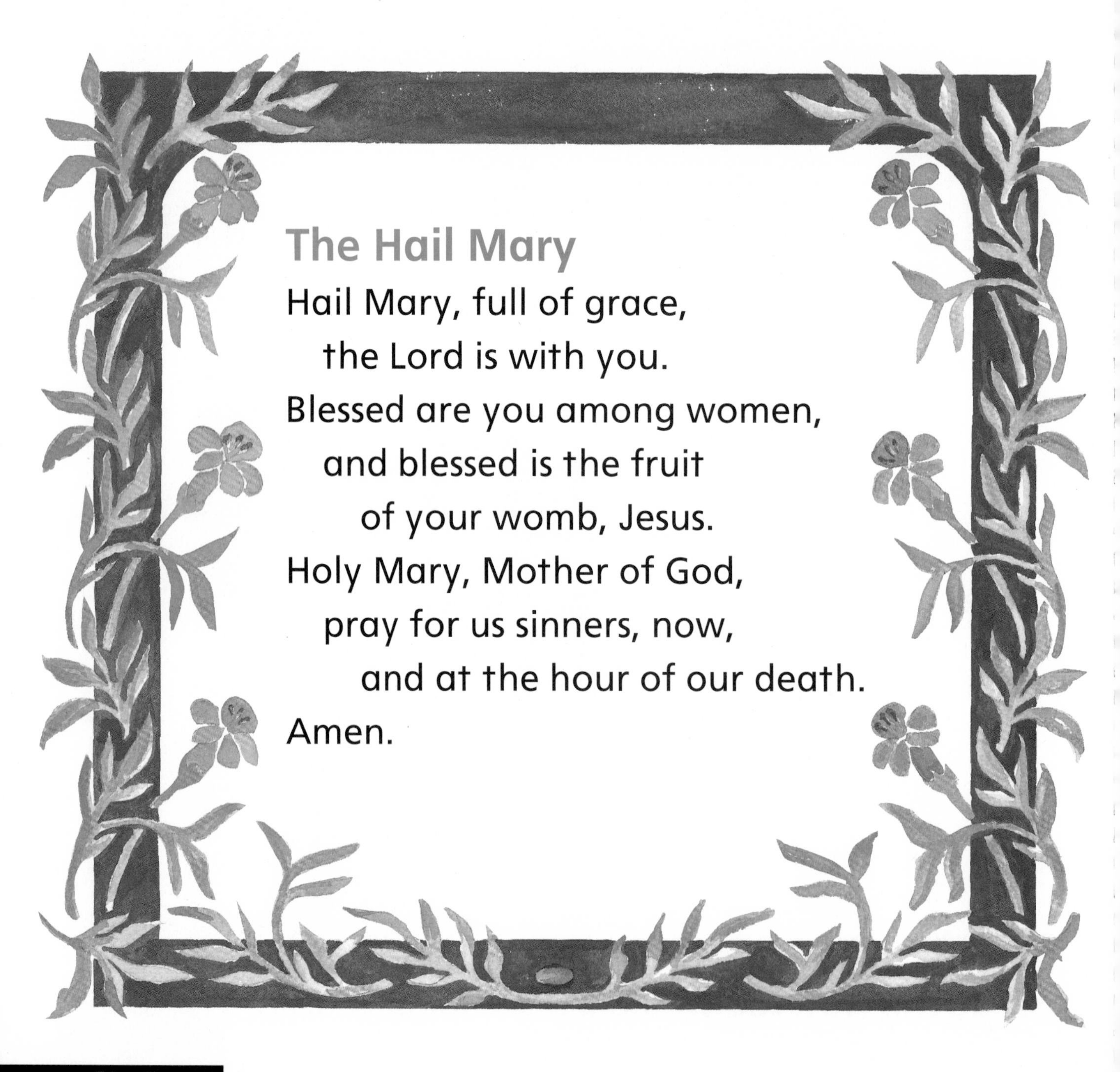

The Hail Mary

Hail Mary, full of grace,
the Lord is with you.
Blessed are you among women,
and blessed is the fruit
of your womb, Jesus.
Holy Mary, Mother of God,
pray for us sinners, now,
and at the hour of our death.
Amen.

Chapter Review

The angel Gabriel brought a message
from God to Mary.
God asked Mary to be the mother of Jesus.
Mary said yes!
Color Mary's answer to show how happy
God, Mary, and the angel Gabriel were.

1. Who is the mother of Jesus?

____

2. With whom does Jesus share his mother?

____

3. Talk about how you can show your love for Mary.

Jesus says, "My mother is your Mother, too."
Based on John 19:27

Jesus Learned Many Things

Children wonder and learn all the time.
What is one thing you would like to learn?

What is one thing you wonder about?

Here are some things that many children like to learn.
Print **YES** on the line before each thing you like to learn.

_____ I like to learn how to play games.

_____ I like to learn how to make things.

_____ I like to learn about animals.

_____ I like to learn new songs.

_____ I like to learn about God.

When Jesus Was a Boy

▲ When you look up at the night sky, what questions do you have?

Jesus listened and asked questions.
Jesus learned about God
and the world around him.
Like Jesus, we can listen and
ask questions.

We Believe

Jesus learned and so can we. We can learn about life and about God. We can ask Jesus to help us learn more about God.

Jesus Liked Learning About God

When Jesus was twelve, Mary and Joseph took him to the **Temple** in Jerusalem. Jesus spent three days with the **rabbis**. These teachers and Jesus talked about life, the Bible, and God. Jesus listened carefully. He amazed the rabbis with his questions. How happy he was to learn more!

Based on Luke 2: 41–47

We Like to Learn About God

Look at each picture.

How are the people learning about God?

What is your favorite way to learn about God's love for you?

New Words

rabbi When Jesus was a boy, a rabbi was someone who taught about God and about life.

Temple The Temple was a holy place in the city of Jerusalem where people prayed and learned about God.

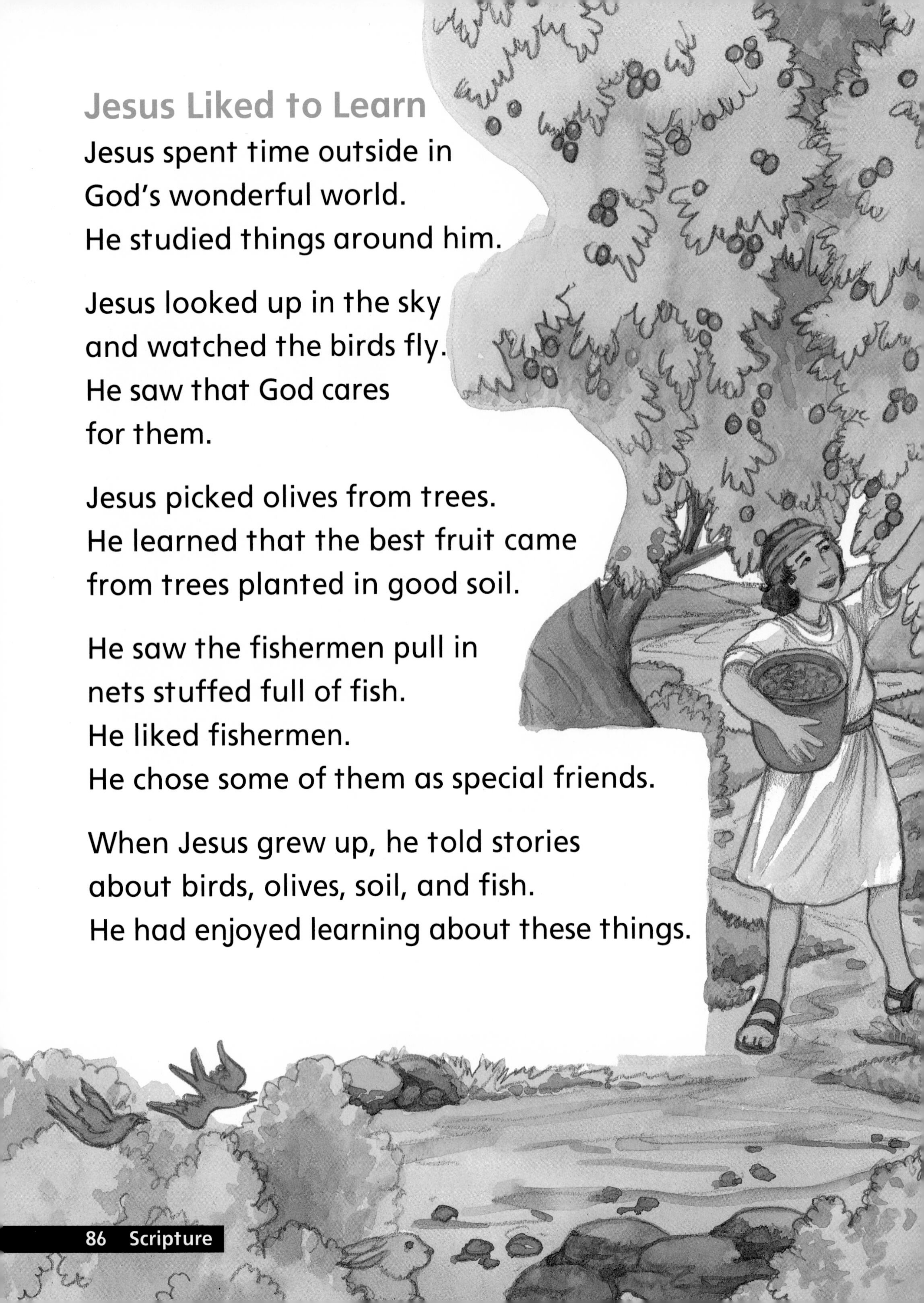

Jesus Liked to Learn

Jesus spent time outside in
God's wonderful world.
He studied things around him.

Jesus looked up in the sky
and watched the birds fly.
He saw that God cares
for them.

Jesus picked olives from trees.
He learned that the best fruit came
from trees planted in good soil.

He saw the fishermen pull in
nets stuffed full of fish.
He liked fishermen.
He chose some of them as special friends.

When Jesus grew up, he told stories
about birds, olives, soil, and fish.
He had enjoyed learning about these things.

We Like to Learn About Our World

Look at the sky.
What do you see?
Rainbows and birds
and leaves on the tree.

Look at the ground!
What do you see?
Brown bugs and worms
and a bumblebee.

And what do we ask when
we see ground and sky?
We ask what and when
and where and why.

And what do we learn
from ground and sky?
We learn God's beauty
is passing by.

Activity

Color all God's gifts you have learned something about.
Circle all God's gifts you have questions about.

We Learn From Signs

When Sarah got on the school bus, she waved to her mother.
That was a good-bye sign.

At lunch time, Sarah saved a seat for Stephen.
That was a sign that they were friends.
But Stephen sat with someone else.
What was that a sign of?

Activity

When Sarah got home from school, she cried.
That was a sign that Sarah was sad about Stephen.

What sign could Sarah's mother give to help her daughter feel better?
What sign could Stephen give to say, "I'm sorry"?

Signs of God

All around us everywhere
Are signs of life
That show God's care.

Activity

Circle the pictures that show signs of God's care.

1.

2.

3.

4.

5.

6.

Praying an Asking Prayer

Jesus sometimes used the psalms to pray.
Like Jesus, we can use the psalms to pray.
We can ask God to help us learn.

Teach me, God, what you want me to know.
Show me your special love.
Help me to learn what you ask of me.

Based on Psalm 119: 33, 41, 73

Chapter Review

Draw a line from Jesus to all the gifts that helped him learn about God and the world. Put an X by the gifts that help you learn.

1. Name one thing Jesus learned about.

2. At the Temple, who helped Jesus learn about life and about God?

3. Talk about ways that you are like Jesus.

Teach me, God, what you want me to know.
Based on Psalm 119:33

Jesus Prayed

Listening and Talking

Whom do you like to talk to?
Whom do you like to listen to?
What do you like to talk about?

Prayer

I said a prayer
And went to bed.
I know God heard
The prayer I said.
My dad told me,
And it is true,
God knows my prayer
Before I do!

What two things do you know about prayer?

Listening and Talking to God

We can talk to God about anything and everything.
God always listens to us.
Talking and listening to God is called **prayer**.

Activity

Look at each picture and answer the question.

▲ What would you say to God about a baby?

▲ What do you want to say to God about your feelings?

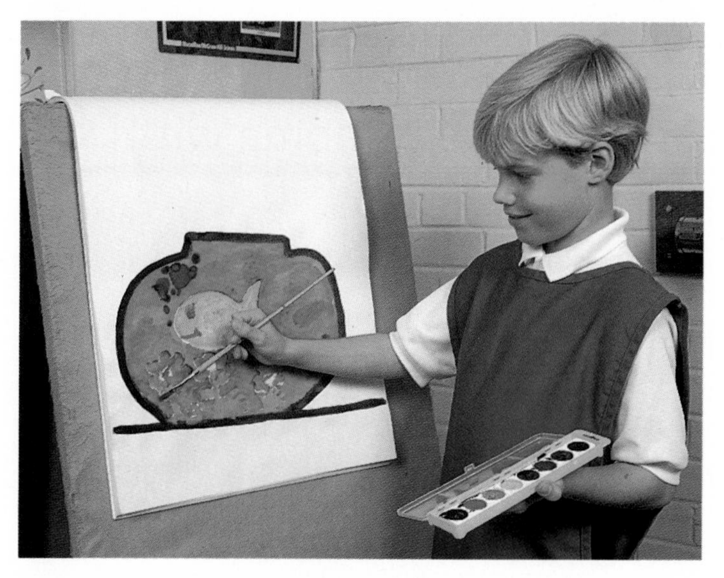

▲ What can you tell God about school?

We Believe

Prayer is talking and listening to God. We grow closer to God when we pray.

New Word

prayer Prayer is listening and talking to God.

Jesus Prayed

Jesus prayed at home with
Mary and Joseph.
He prayed in the morning.
He prayed in the evening.
He always prayed at meals.
He prayed with others
and alone.

Jesus prayed anytime and
everywhere.
Because he loved God, his
Father, Jesus liked to pray .

Activity

Like Jesus, we are called to love God.
We, too, can talk and listen to God.
Put an **X** next to each time and
place you like to pray.

☐ outside

☐ inside

☐ in the morning

☐ in the evening

☐ at meals

☐ in church

Talking to God

We can talk to God about many things.

Activity

Below are some things that people tell God
when they pray.
Think of a time you said one of these things to God.

Draw a picture of that time.
Then draw a line to connect the prayer to your picture.

Kinds of Prayer

Jesus talked to God about many things.
Jesus often used his own words to pray.
Sometimes Jesus prayed the psalms
that are from the Bible.
Here are some kinds of prayers he said.

O Lord, my God,
you are great and good.

Based on Psalm 104:1

Praise

I will give thanks to you,
O Lord, with all my heart.

Based on Psalm 9:2

Thanks

Listen to me, O Lord,
and be my helper.

Based on Psalm 30:11

Help

I love you, O Lord.
You keep me safe.

Based on Psalm 18:2, 4

Love

Activity

Roberto gets ready for school each day.
Look at all the things he does.
Put an **X** next to each thing you do
to get ready for school.

☐ Check on the weather report.

☐ Comb your hair.

☐ Pack your books.

☐ Put out your clothes.

Getting Ready to Pray

Winona wants to pray.
She gets ready to talk and listen to God.

She finds a quiet place to pray.

Winona makes the Sign of the Cross.

She tries to think only about God.

Winona talks to God about the beautiful world.

Praying with God's Gifts

God loves us and give us many gifts.

When we pray, we can hold one of God's gifts.

The gift will remind us of God's love.

The gift will help us to be quiet inside.

Activity

Circle one of the gifts you would like to hold
as you talk to God.

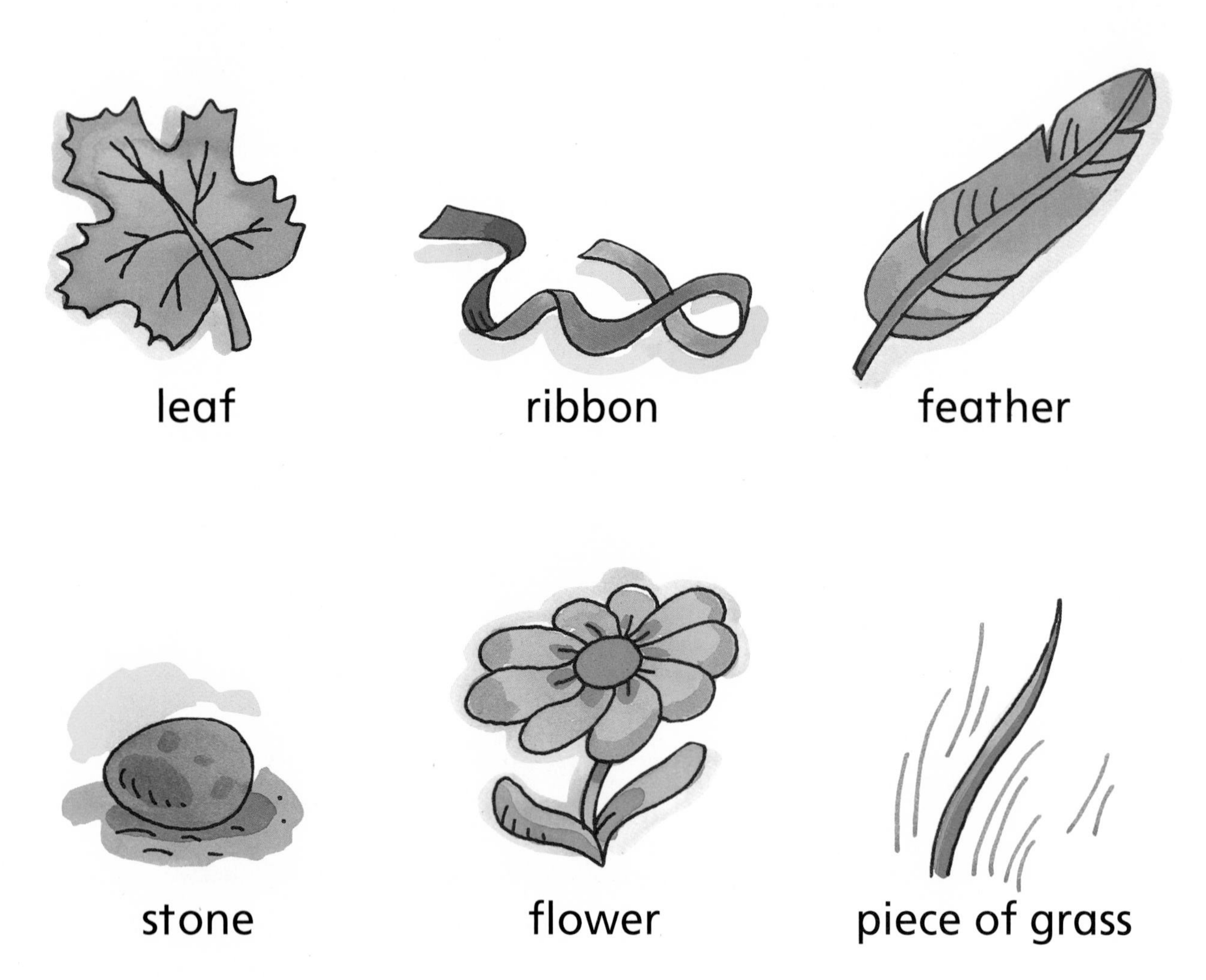

Chapter Review

Cross out all the **R** letters.

R	R	I	R	R	C	A	N	R	R	T	A	L	K	R	R	T	O	R	R	G	O	D	R	R

What message can you read?

Copy the message below.

____

1. What do we call listening and talking to God?

____

2. Where can we pray?

____

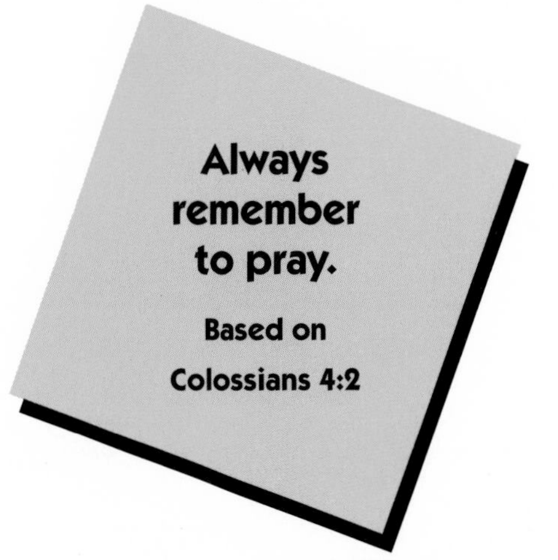

3. Talk about when, why, and where you pray.

Unit 2 Organizer

Finish the words.

W______ together

P______ together

The Holy Family

L ______ from one another

L ______ each other

Unit 2 Review

Draw a line to match the words with their meanings.

1. The Holy Family •	• messenger from God
2. Angel •	• Jesus' hometown
3. Nazareth •	• Jesus' family

Circle the correct word to complete each sentence.

1. Joseph was a _____.
   doctor carpenter
2. _____ is the mother of Jesus.
   Mary Gabriel
3. Jesus' teachers were called _____.
   holy men rabbis
4. The _____ is a place where people pray.
   hall Temple
5. Jesus learned to pray _____ and everywhere.
   sometimes anytime
6. _____ is listening and praying to God.
   Baptism Prayer

Unit 2 Review

Look at the pictures below.
Fill in the first letter of each word.

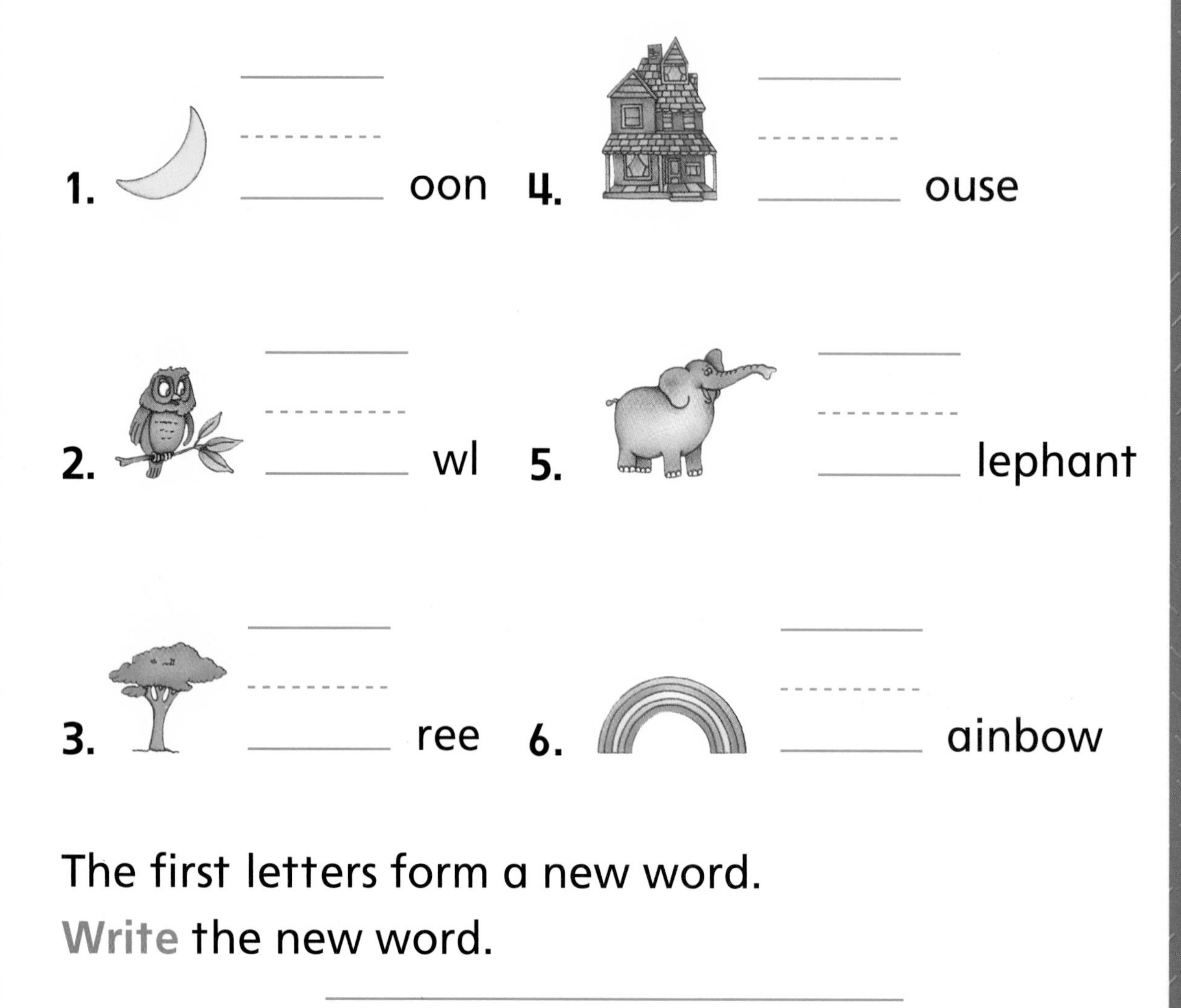

The first letters form a new word.
Write the new word.

Mary is our ______________.

BECOMING A FEELINGS DETECTIVE

We can discover how others feel. We can look and listen.

Activity

Each picture below shows a different feeling.
Look for the clues in the pictures that tell how
Boots and Zip are feeling.
Match the "feeling" words to the correct pictures.

1. Happy 2. Shy 3. Angry 4. Proud

Activity

Here are more "feeling" words and pictures to match.
Be a good Feelings Detective!

1. Worried 2. Sad 3. Embarrassed

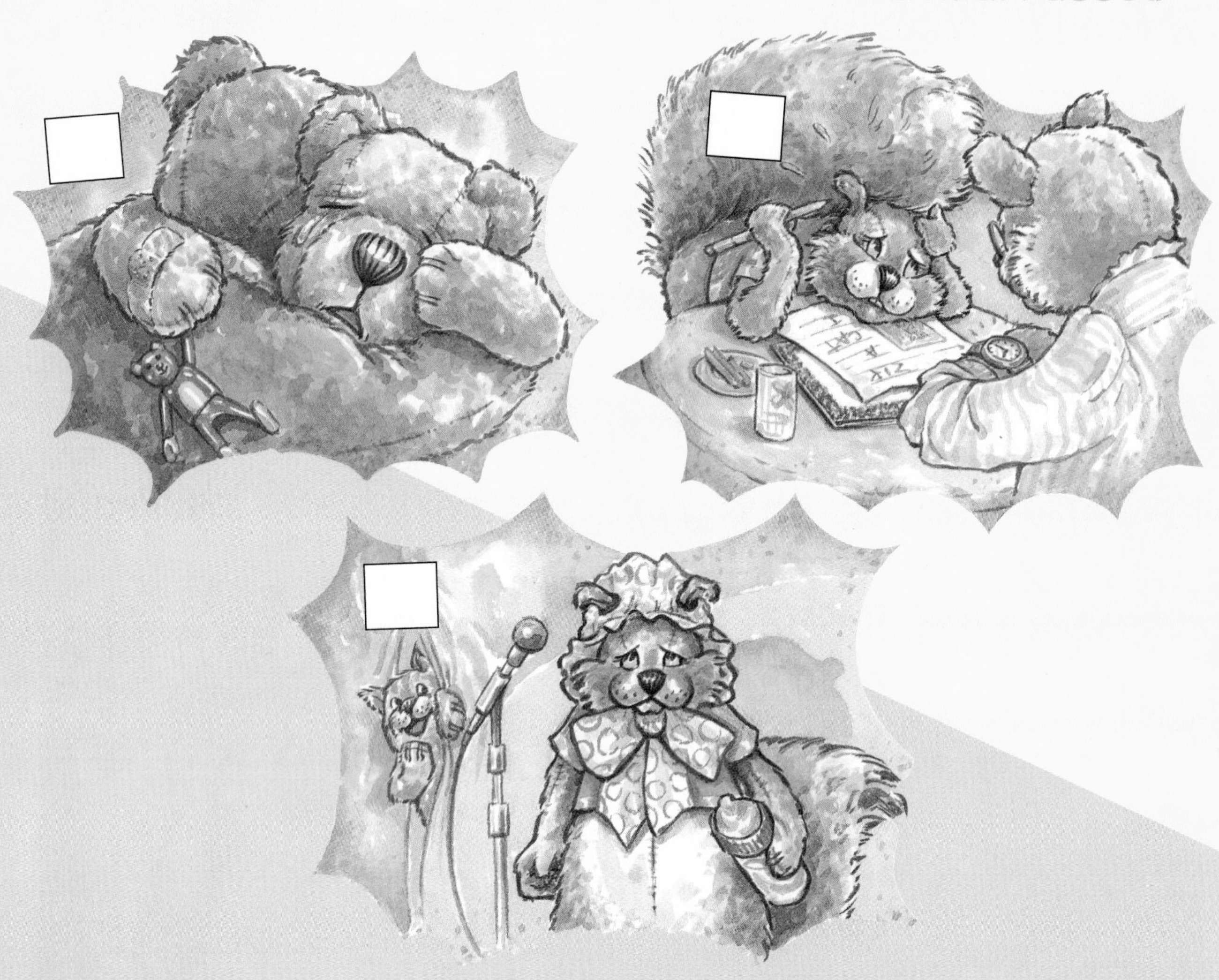

Following Jesus

Jesus asks us to care about people.
Knowing how someone feels helps us to care.
We can tell how someone feels by

LOOKING and **LISTENING**.

Growing Closer

FIND THE BOOK OF PSALMS in the Old Testament section of the Bible. Read a few psalms, either alone or to your family. Then, write your own family "psalms." Psalms can express praise, thanks, sorrow, or petition. Use your "psalms" as meal prayers or bedtime prayers.

AS A FAMILY, discover one way you can all learn more about God. Try reading the Scriptures together, discussing a topic such as prayer, or joining Bible classes for children and adults in your parish.

Looking Ahead

To help your child realize the importance of caring for ourselves and others, Unit 3 focuses on Jesus' teaching and example. Your child will learn that prayer is one expression of caring that Jesus lived and taught. He or she will also learn the Our Father and will consider the meaning of this prayer in our daily lives.

OPENING DOORS

A Take-Home Magazine™

A Closer Look

Praise the Word of the Lord!

When we were young, we were taught to be respectful. Standing when introduced to a dignitary, offering our seat on the bus to an elderly person, or holding the door open were ways we learned to show deference. Catholics have always esteemed certain people, places, and things because they are of God. One of those things that we hold sacred is the Bible. Over the centuries, we honored God's word and developed traditions to show reverence for the Scriptures, especially when they are read at Sunday Mass. These rituals are described below.

The Scripture readings are in the Lectionary. The book called a Lectionary contains all the Scripture readings for Mass. It is sometimes covered elaborately to show the regard we have for God's word.

The Lectionary has a special place. Believing that the Lectionary contains the message of Jesus, we carry it in procession to the lectern. In many parishes, the book is displayed on the front ledge of the lectern where it can be reverenced throughout the week.

We sing "Alleluia." To prepare ourselves to hear the message of Jesus, we sing Alleluia, which means "Praise the Lord."

Ordinarily, the opinion of women was unsolicited, but Luke includes the responses of three women to highlight Jesus' sense of the importance of women. Mary, the faithful handmaiden, becomes the mother of the Savior. Elizabeth, her cousin and John the Baptizer's mother, acknowledges the presence of Jesus in Mary's womb. Anna, the aged prophetess in the Temple, is together with Simeon the symbol of the faithful Jewish people who longed for the Messiah.

You can see from these examples that Luke brought together many stories and Old Testament prophecies to help the early Christians better understand Jesus. Matthew, too, used the infancy narratives to interpret the meaning of Jesus. Writing for the many Christian Jews that existed in his time, Matthew opens his gospel with a genealogy of Jesus. Designating Jesus as "the son of David," the author establishes the newborn infant as the anticipated royal Messiah. Matthew highlights the childhood suffering of Jesus—the persecution by Herod and the subsequent flight into Egypt. For Jesus' Jewish audience, these stories depict Jesus as reliving the experiences of the People of Israel. The Holy Family takes refuge in Egypt as their ancestors did many generations ago, and like Moses, Jesus is called out of Egypt to save the people.

Although we do not discover many facts about the childhood of Jesus from the infancy narratives, we can learn much about Jesus.

The Childhood of Jesus

Christians have always been curious about the childhood of Jesus. We love to imagine Jesus helping Joseph in the carpenter shop or drawing water for Mary at the well. Actually the Bible tells us nothing of these kinds of facts. Even such familiar things as the manger scene imprinted on our Christmas cards have much more meaning than meets the eye.

Why are details about Jesus' early life so noticeably absent from the gospels? The reason is that the authors did not intend to draft biographies of the baby Jesus but rather to answer questions such as "Is Jesus really the Messiah?" or "Can Jesus really be God if he was born here on earth? Two gospels tell of the event surrounding the birth and early childhood of Jesus in stories that we call infancy narratives: Matthew 1:1–2:23 and Luke 1:5–2:52

Addressing the question, "Who is Jesus Christ?" Luke portrays the joy and peace associated with the Savior's coming to earth. "On earth peace to those on whom his favor rests," proclaims the heavenly host the first Christmas night (Luke 2:14).

Luke also shows Jesus' concern for the poor and the lowly in the infancy narratives. It was no accident that the lowly shepherds were the first to behold the newborn Savior. They are signs for us all that God favors the poor and the lowly.

We incense the book. Sometimes, incense is used, and on those occasions, the book containing the gospels is reverenced.

A special minister proclaims the gospel. To emphasize the importance of the gospel, a special minister—the deacon—reads the gospel. When no deacon is available, the priest proclaims the gospel.

We have an "honor guard." At times ministers, often servers, stand with lighted candles to honor the words of Jesus. You have probably seen this on festive days such as Christmas.

We stand for the reading of the gospel. Standing has long been considered a sign of respect. While we sit for the other readings during the Liturgy of the Word, we stand to hear Jesus' message.

God's word is praised. At the end of the gospel, the deacon or priest says,
"The word of the Lord."
We respond,
"Praise to you, Lord Jesus Christ."

We venerate the gospel book. At Mass both the altar and the gospel book are kissed by the priest. This action is a sign that both the table and the word are signs of the presence of Jesus.

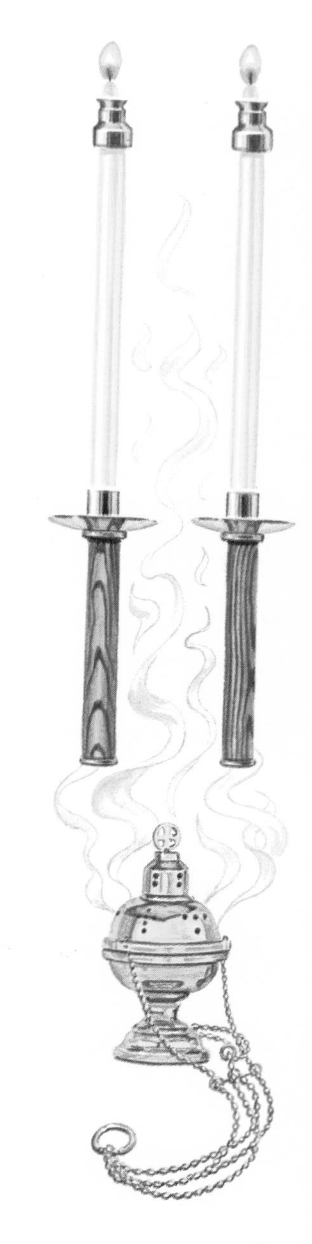

Learning More About God

The Liturgy of the Word contains several distinct yet related parts. These pages will focus on two of these parts: the responsorial psalm and the homily. Read these pages with your child and talk about the illustrations. Help your child complete the activity.

Read Along

When Jesus was about my age, Mary and Joseph took him to the Temple to pray. Jesus probably prayed special prayers called psalms.

When I go to Mass with my family, I pray the psalms, too. Sometimes I say the psalm aloud. Sometimes I sing it.

At the Temple, the rabbis and Jesus talked about God. Together, they read stories from the Bible. Then the rabbis and Jesus discussed what those stories meant.

At Mass I hear stories from the Bible, too. The priest or deacon helps me understand what the stories mean. This is called the homily.

I try to listen carefully. I want to learn more about God, just as Jesus did!

Circle the pictures of people who help you learn more about God.

Pray the responsorial psalm with the priest and people the next time you go to Mass. Listen carefully to the homily.

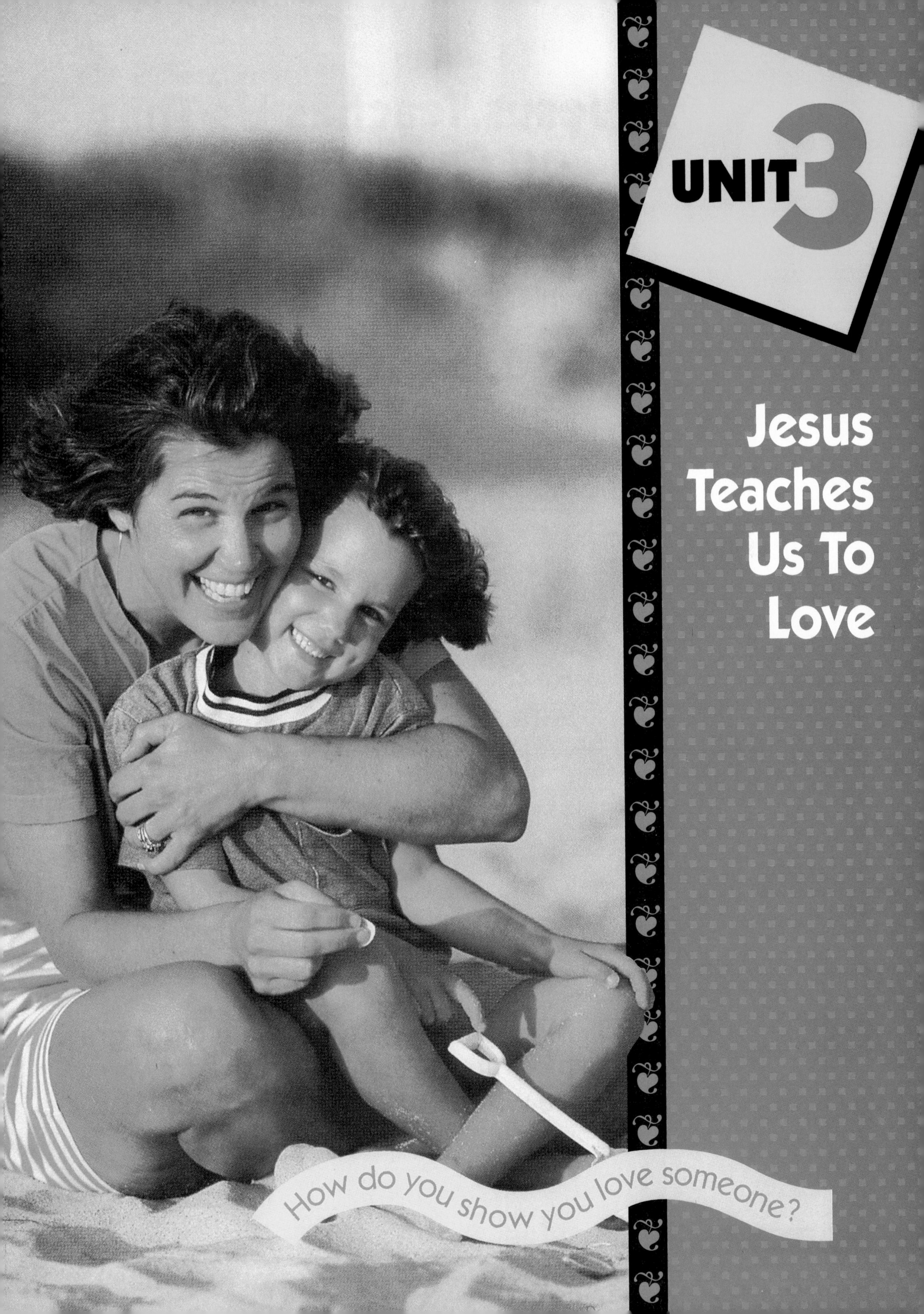
UNIT 3
Jesus Teaches Us To Love
How do you show you love someone?

9

Jesus Teaches Us That God Cares

All Things Need Care

People, animals, and plants need care.

1. Mike planted a seed.
He covered it with dirt.

2. Joan watered the seed.
Soon she saw a tiny plant.

3. Mike put the tiny plant in the sun.
He watched and waited.

4. The plant grew and grew.
One day a flower bloomed.

What are the names of some people and things that need care?

Activity

Circle the ways you can care for animals.

God Cares for All Things

God knows what plants and animals need.

God knows what we need, too.

Activity

Draw something that you need to be healthy.

Jesus Teaches Us About God, His Father

One sunny day many people sat
on a hillside with Jesus.
Jesus pointed to birds in the sky.
He said, "Look at the birds!
God cares for them and feeds them.
But you are more important
than the birds.
God, your Father, cares even more about you."

Then Jesus said, "Look at the flowers.
How beautiful they are!
But you are more beautiful than
these flowers.
God, your Father, cares much more for each
of you."

Based on Matthew 6:26-30

Jesus tells us that God cares for everyone.
We **trust** God to care for us and
for all creation.
We are most like God when we care
for each other and all creation.

We Believe

Jesus teaches us that God the Father cares for all living things. God cares for people most of all.

New Word

trust Trust means to believe in someone's love for us.

God Cares for All Creation

God takes good care of the earth.
God creates bugs.
Worms wiggle to make good dirt.
Then roses bloom for us to enjoy.

God takes good care of plants.
God's sun shines in the sky.
God's rain falls on the ground.
Then carrots and other food grow
for us to eat.

God takes good care of animals.
God clothes the animals with fur.
Then the cats and dogs can stay
warm in the winter.

God takes good care of all of us.
God dresses the mountains with trees.
Then maples and evergreen trees
clean the air for us to breathe.
God takes good care of us.

Activity

Make a chart of some of the things
in God's creation.
Count the things that God cares for.

- ☐ Bugs
- ☐ Fruits & Vegetables
- ☐ Flowers
- ☐ Birds
- ☐ Animals
- ☐ People

Caring for God's Creation

One day three first graders saw the city dump filled with garbage. "Some of this junk can harm our earth. Let's do something about it," Luis said. "Let's help God take care of the world."

Brian said. "I'll take care of my toys so they won't break."
When he grew too old for his toys, Brian gave them to other children to use.

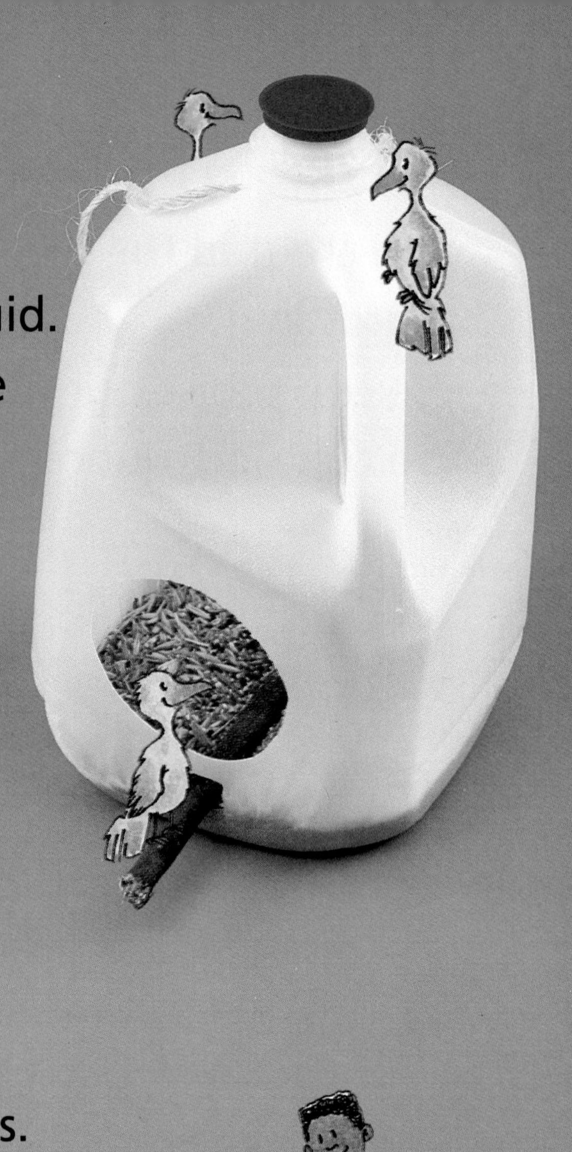

Kate drank lots of milk.
Then she had a wonderful idea.
"I could make a bird feeder," she said.
She cut an opening in a milk bottle
and hung the bird feeder from
a tree limb.
Kate did not make garbage.
Instead, she made a feeder
for God's birds.

At the beach, Luis saw a piece of
plastic with six rings to hold cans.
"A little fish could get caught
in the rings and die," Luis said.
So he snipped the rings with scissors.
That way the garbage could not
hurt any fish or animals.

Activity

Look at the pictures and
think about the stories.
Circle what you will do.

Praying a Prayer of Praise

God created the world and all
that is in it.
We can praise our good God.
We can sing, dance, and play instruments.

Praise God in the heavens!
Praise God for creation!
Praise God with the trumpet!
Praise God with the harp!
Praise God with song and dance!
Praise God with cymbals!
Let all creation praise God!

Based on Psalm 150

Chapter Review

Activity

God cares for all creation.

Show how you can care for God's creation, too.

Put the pictures below in 1, 2, 3 order.

1. Who cares for all creation?

2. What word means to believe in someone's love for us?

3. Talk about how God cares for people and all creation.

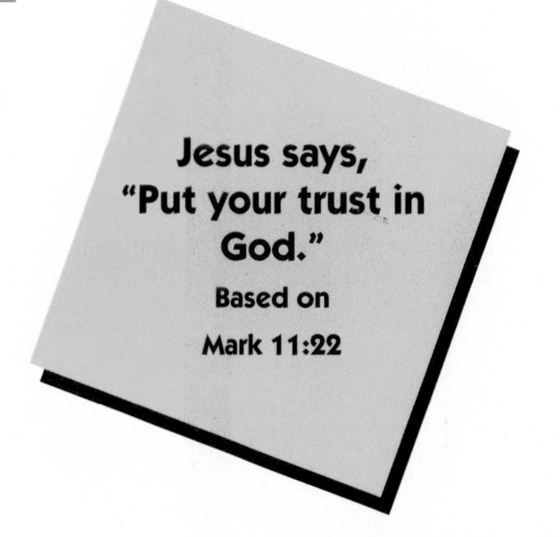

10

Jesus Cares for Us

What are some ways that people show you they care about you?

Caring People

Tell a story about each picture.

Look at the people being cared for.

How do they feel?

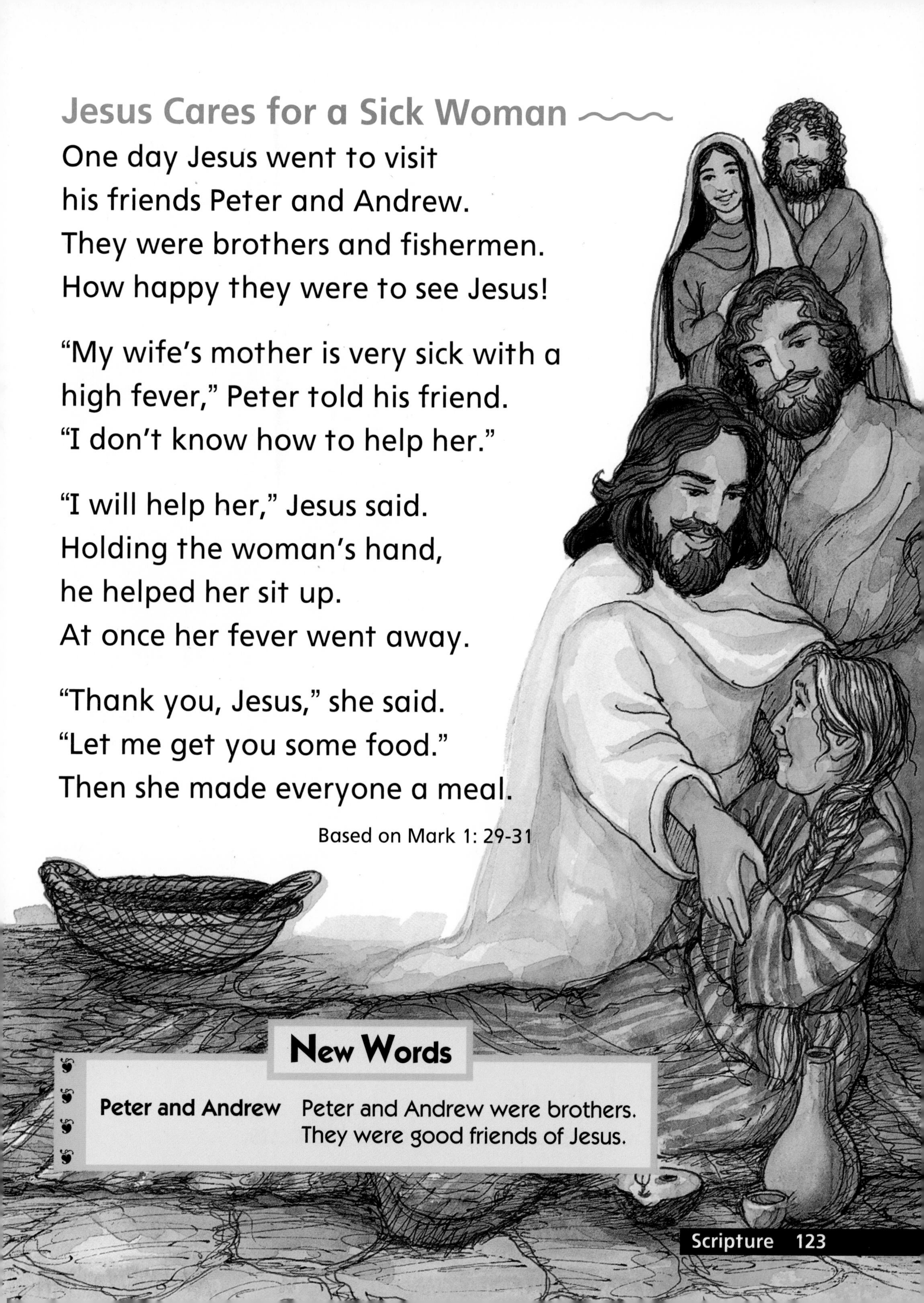

Jesus Cares for a Sick Woman

One day Jesus went to visit
his friends Peter and Andrew.
They were brothers and fishermen.
How happy they were to see Jesus!

"My wife's mother is very sick with a
high fever," Peter told his friend.
"I don't know how to help her."

"I will help her," Jesus said.
Holding the woman's hand,
he helped her sit up.
At once her fever went away.

"Thank you, Jesus," she said.
"Let me get you some food."
Then she made everyone a meal.

Based on Mark 1: 29-31

New Words

Peter and Andrew	Peter and Andrew were brothers. They were good friends of Jesus.

Counting on Someone

We can trust some people
to do their best to help us.
They try to keep their promises to us.
They often know what is good for us.

Read the stories below.

"Daddy, thank you for
keeping your promise and
taking me to the zoo." ▶

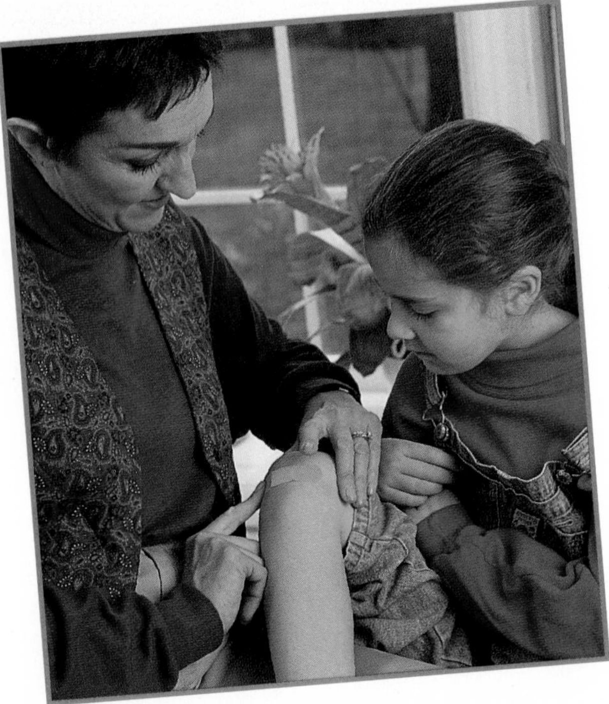

◀ "I will put a bandage
on your cut."
"I am glad I was
here to help you."

We Can Trust Jesus

We can count on Jesus to love and help us.
Remember, Jesus is always with us.

Activity

This story is about Jesus and a man who trusted him.

One day Jesus and his friend went walking.

They met a man who was blind.

The blind man trusted Jesus.

"Help me see, Jesus," he said.

Based on Mark 10:46

Draw what you think happened.

Jesus Cares for Us

Jesus cared for Andrew, Peter,
and Peter's mother-in-law.
He cared for the blind man.

Jesus cares for everyone.
He loves us and is always with us.
One way Jesus cares for us is
through the loving care of others.

A Caring Woman

This play is about Elizabeth Seton,
who cared for many children.

We have no home, no place to live.

Come with me, I will make a home for you.

We want to learn to read, but we have no schools.

My sisters and I will teach you. Come with us.

We are hungry, but we have no money for food and milk.

I will ask Jesus to help me, and I will find food and milk for you.

Jesus never forgets us. Elizabeth Seton's love shows Jesus' love.

Activity

These are the names of people who care for me.

We Believe

Jesus loves and cares for everyone. One way Jesus cares for people today is through caring people. We must care for others also.

People Can Show Jesus' Love

Emily plays games with Tim.
He knows that Jesus is loving him through Emily.
How does Tim feel when his sister cares for him as Jesus showed us?

Grandpa O'Mara takes Tara fishing.
Tara knows that Jesus is loving her through Grandpa.
How does Tara feel when Grandpa cares for her just as Jesus calls us to?

Aunt Ramona bakes cookies for Carlos.
Carlos knows that Jesus is loving him through Aunt Ramona.
How does Carlos feel when his aunt cares for him as Jesus wants?

Mr. Ling bandages Chun's knee.
Chun knows that Jesus is caring for him through Mr. Ling.
How does Chun feel when her neighbor cares for her as Jesus showed us?

Activity

Draw lines to match the pictures that go together. Then tell what you think the children might say to the people who care for them.

Praying With Bible Stories

When we gather to pray, we can remember Jesus' love. To help us, we can retell some Bible stories we know about Jesus. Here are some different ways to tell a story we know.

- We can pantomime it.
- We can draw pictures of it.
- We can make up a dance that retells the story.

Choose one of these ways to tell a story of Jesus' love.

Chapter Review

Activity

Many special people love us and care for us. To discover who loves us the most, color the spaces that have an X in them.

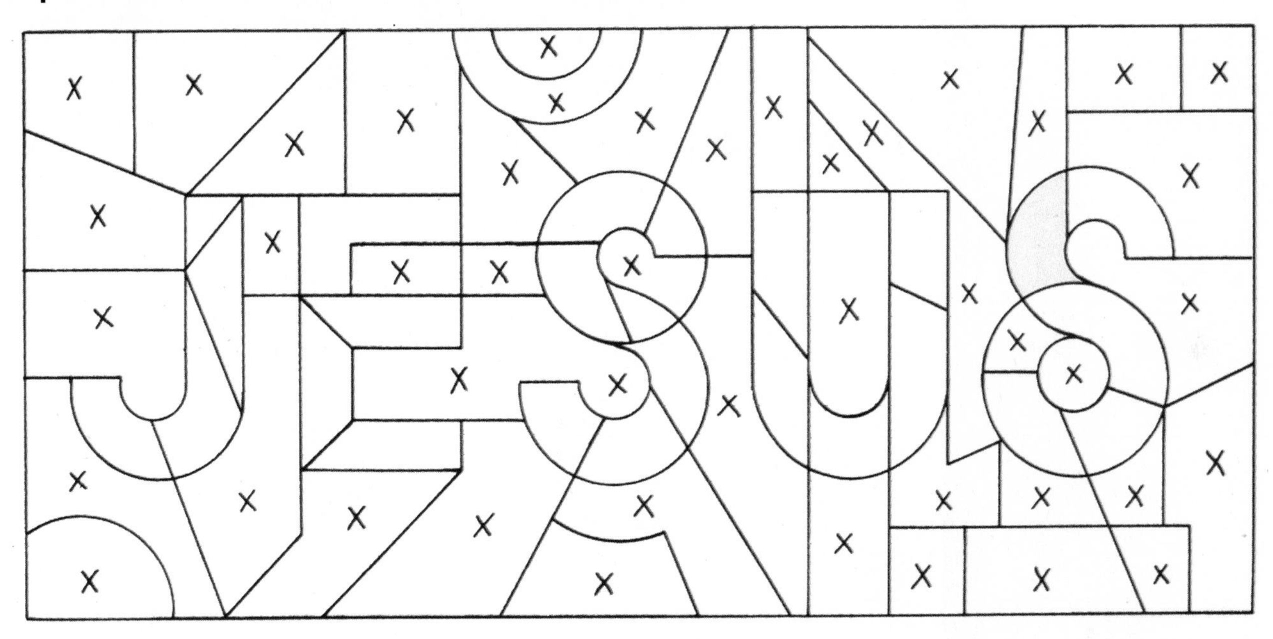

1. Which two brothers were friends of Jesus?

2. Who cured the woman in the Bible story?

Jesus loves me.
Based on Galatians 2:20

3. Talk about ways that Jesus cares for you through caring people.

Jesus Teaches Us to Care

Who Cares?

"I care!"
The mother says,
When she hears
A baby cry.

"I care!"
The gardener says,
When he sees
The plants are dry.

"I care!"
The teacher says,
When a student
Doesn't know.

"I care!"
The Creator says,
"For all that
Lives and grows."

What is one thing that you do for someone that shows you care?

Jesus Asks Us to Help

Jesus wants us to care for the world. Jesus teaches us to care for people who need help.

Activity

Jesus teaches us to take care of God's world.
Circle all the people in the picture who are caring for God's creation.

We Believe

Jesus teaches us to care for people who need help.

The Good Samaritan

One day someone said to Jesus,
"God says we must love our neighbor.
But who is my neighbor?"
Jesus answered by telling this story
about the **Good Samaritan**.

A man was walking down a road.
Some robbers jumped out of the bushes.
They stole his money and clothes.
Then they beat him up.

A leader of the people passed by.
He saw the man but did not stop.

Next, a helper from the Temple came by.
He too saw the man but did not stop.

Finally, a Samaritan saw the man.
The Samaritan washed the man's wounds.
The Samaritan gave the man some
clothes and took the man to an inn
for food and rest.

Then Jesus asked, "Which person in this
story acted like a neighbor to the man
who was robbed?"

Based on Luke 10:25-36

Activity

How would you answer Jesus?

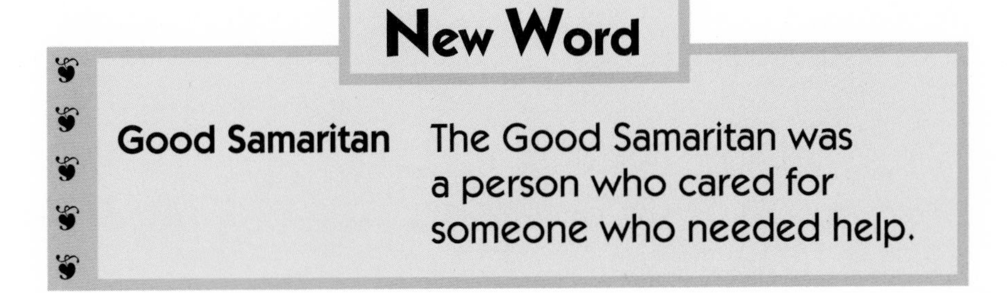

New Word

Good Samaritan The Good Samaritan was a person who cared for someone who needed help.

Being Good Samaritans

Jesus wants us to care for others.

We can care for plants, animals, and people.

We can find many ways to care for others.

Activity

Play the game that follows.

1. You will need a coin and a button.
2. Flip the coin to see how many spaces to move the button.

Heads=1 space

Tails=2 spaces

2

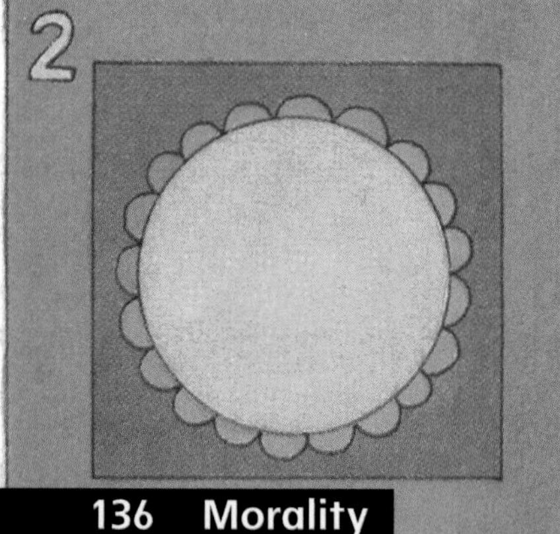

3 You said, NO

to someone who needed help.

Go back to **START**.

4

Activity

Choose a word to complete each sentence.

1. A good neighbor is kind and

_______________________ people.

2. Jesus wants me to be a

_______________________ neighbor.

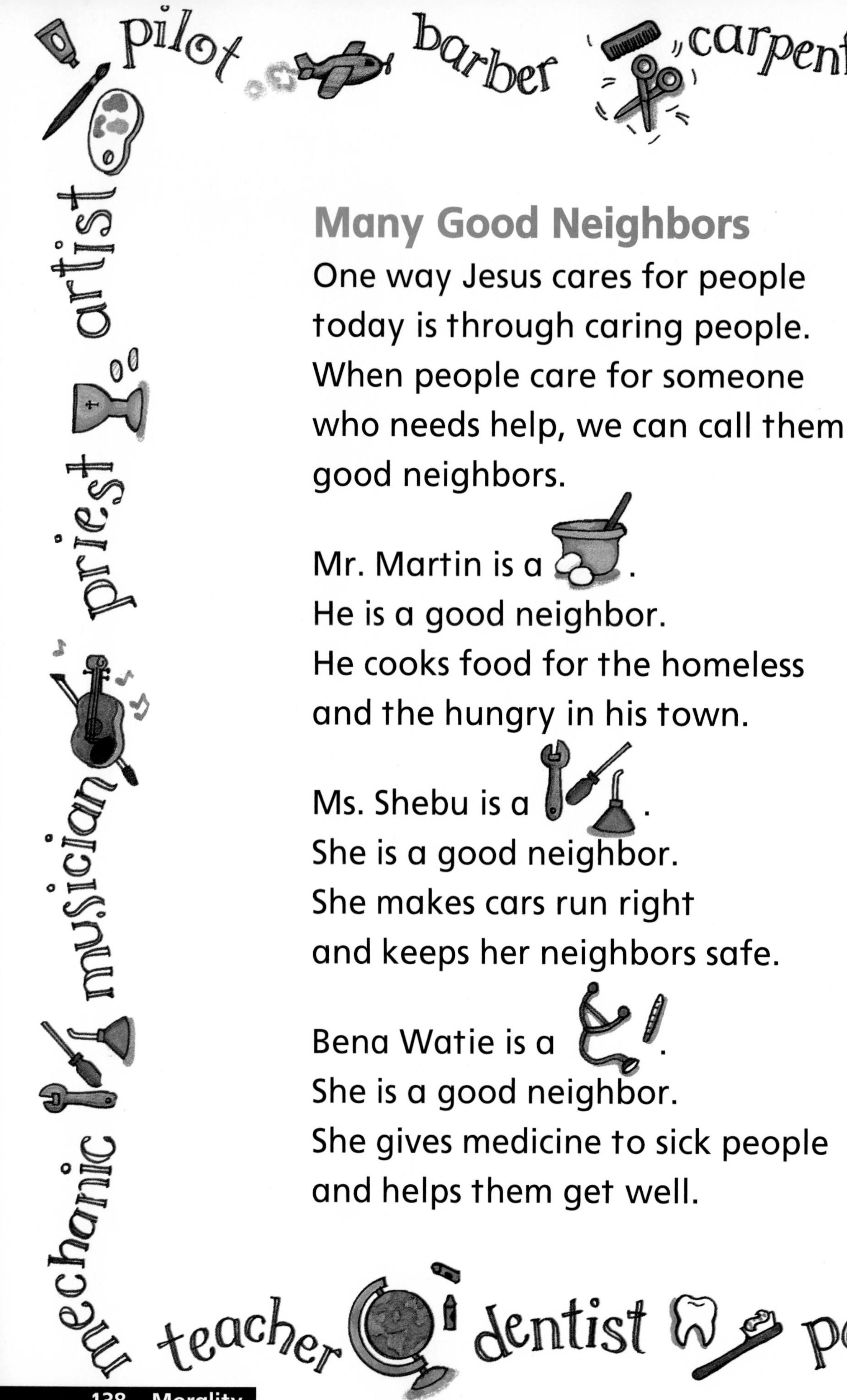

Many Good Neighbors

One way Jesus cares for people today is through caring people. When people care for someone who needs help, we can call them good neighbors.

Mr. Martin is a [cook].
He is a good neighbor.
He cooks food for the homeless and the hungry in his town.

Ms. Shebu is a [mechanic].
She is a good neighbor.
She makes cars run right and keeps her neighbors safe.

Bena Watie is a [doctor].
She is a good neighbor.
She gives medicine to sick people and helps them get well.

cook mailcarrier doctor farmer firefighter librarian nurse

Taro Uno is a .
He is a good neighbor.
He teaches children about God's world and helps them learn to read and write.

Mrs. Ming is a .
She is a good neighbor.
She loves her two children and listens to their stories.

Mr. Johnson is a .
He is a good neighbor.
He raises food for us to eat and is kind to animals.

When these people care,
they are being good neighbors.

Praying with a Play

There are many ways to think over the stories from the Bible.
We can act out the story.
Putting on a play helps us remember the story.
We can imagine what happened and what people said.

You might want to put on a play about the Good Samaritan.

Chapter Review

Activity

Choose one of the objects.
Tell how you can use it to be a good neighbor.

1. In Jesus' story, who acted like a good neighbor?

2. Who teaches us to care for others?

3. Talk about how you can help other people.

Jesus says, "Love one another as I love you."
Based on John 15:12

Jesus Teaches Us to Pray

What Are These People Doing?

Whom are they listening and talking to?

What is your favorite way of praying?

Sometimes when
I am by myself,
Alone and thinking quietly,
I talk to God, my special friend,
Or listen as God talks to me.

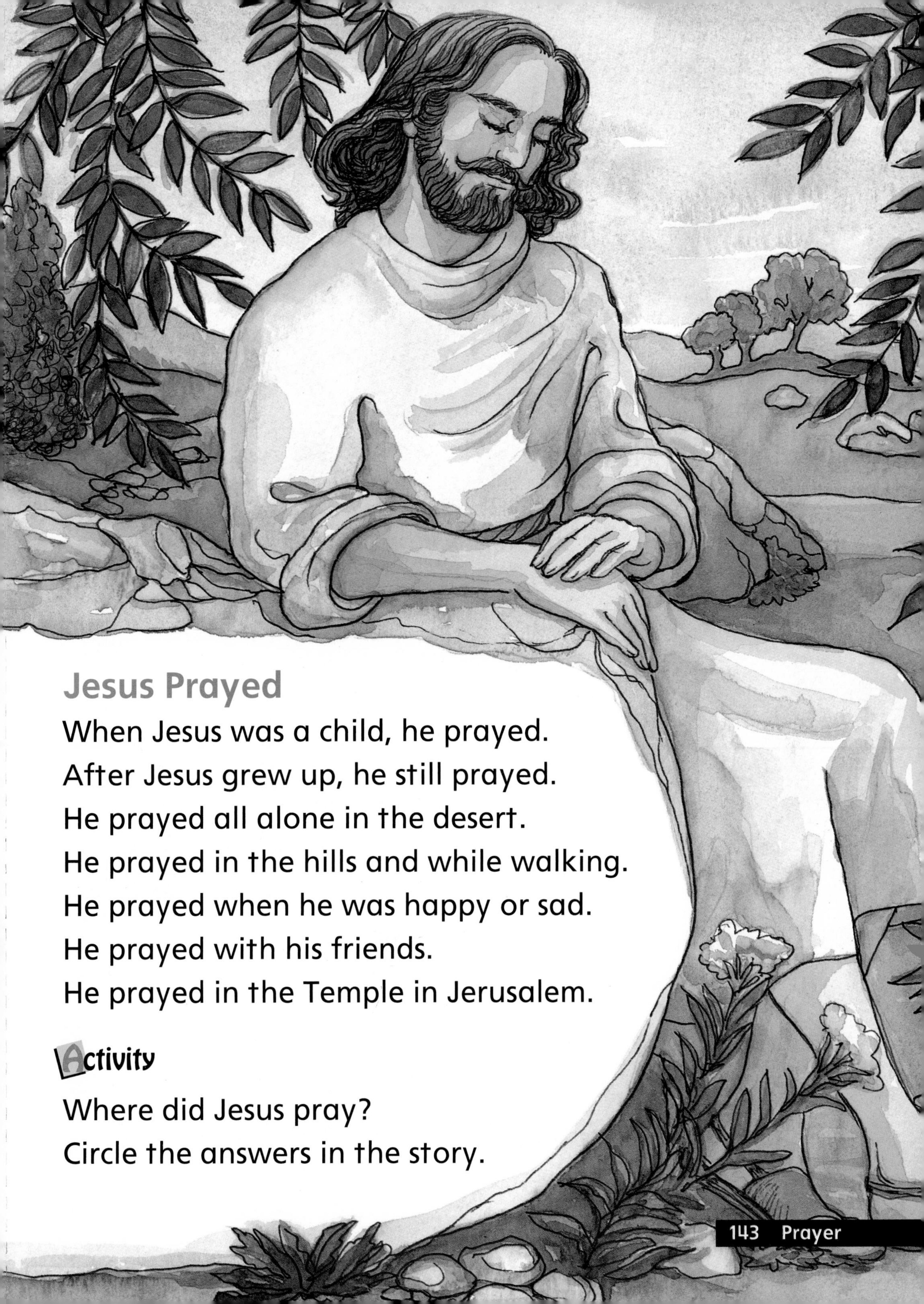

Jesus Prayed

When Jesus was a child, he prayed.
After Jesus grew up, he still prayed.
He prayed all alone in the desert.
He prayed in the hills and while walking.
He prayed when he was happy or sad.
He prayed with his friends.
He prayed in the Temple in Jerusalem.

Activity

Where did Jesus pray?
Circle the answers in the story.

The Lord's Prayer

Jesus' friends often saw him pray.
They knew he liked to talk
and listen to God, his Father.

One day, Jesus' friends said,
"Please, Jesus, teach us how to pray."
So Jesus taught them this prayer.

Our Father, who art in heaven,
 hallowed be thy name;
thy kingdom come;
thy will be done on earth—
 as it is in **heaven**.
Give us this day our daily bread;
and forgive us our trespasses
 as we forgive those
 who **trespass** against us;
and lead us not into temptation,
 but deliver us from evil.
Amen.

Based on Matthew 6:9-13

New Words

hallowed Hallowed means holy.

heaven Heaven is being happy with God forever.

trespass Trespass means to hurt someone.

We Believe

Jesus prayed and teaches us to pray.

Activity

The words below mean "God" in different languages. Circle the pictures that show the word "God" in a language you can speak or would like to learn.

God Our Father

Jesus, the Son of God, prayed.
Jesus taught all of us to pray.
He taught us to say "Our Father."
Why did Jesus say "Our Father"
instead of "My Father?"

Jesus wants us to know that
God is our Father, too.
Jesus wants us to remember that
God loves everyone.

Circle one group of words in each line.
Make up a prayer to say to God.

God	Our Father	Our Creator
You give me	You care for	You created
my friends	my family	the world
with love.	always.	because you are so good.

Write your prayer on the lines below.

Praying Jesus' Prayer

We Christians live everywhere.
All of us pray The Lord's Prayer.
Look at the map and the pictures.
See how Christians everywhere
pray The Lord's Prayer.

What does The Lord's Prayer mean?

1. **Our Father, who art in heaven**

   Who is "Our Father"?

2. **Give us this day our daily bread**

   What does this mean?

   Circle the correct picture.

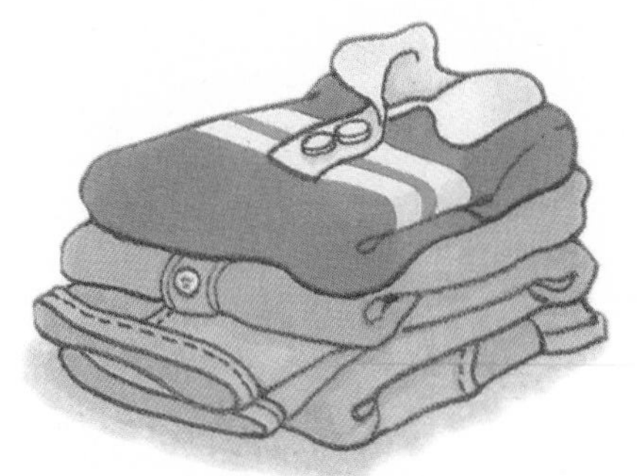

3. **And forgive us our trespasses as we forgive those who trespass against us**

   Show what it means by putting an **X** by the correct picture.

Praying with Actions

Our Father,
who art in heaven,
hallowed be thy name;

thy kingdom come;
thy will be done on earth
as it is in heaven.

Give us this day
our daily bread;

and forgive us our trespasses
as we forgive those
who trespass against us;

and lead us not
into temptation,
but deliver us from evil.
Amen

Chapter Review

1. When we pray The Lord's Prayer, we know God cares for us. ____________________

   God asks us to ____________________ for others.

2. We know God forgives us. ____________________

   God asks us to ____________________ others.

1. What prayer did Jesus teach us?

   ____

2. Whom do we pray to?

   ____

3. Talk about times when you pray The Lord's Prayer.

Keep on praying with a thankful heart.
Based on Colossians 4:2

Unit 3 Organizer

Jesus Teaches Us

To ______________________

for other living things.

To ______________________

one another.

To ______________________

for people.

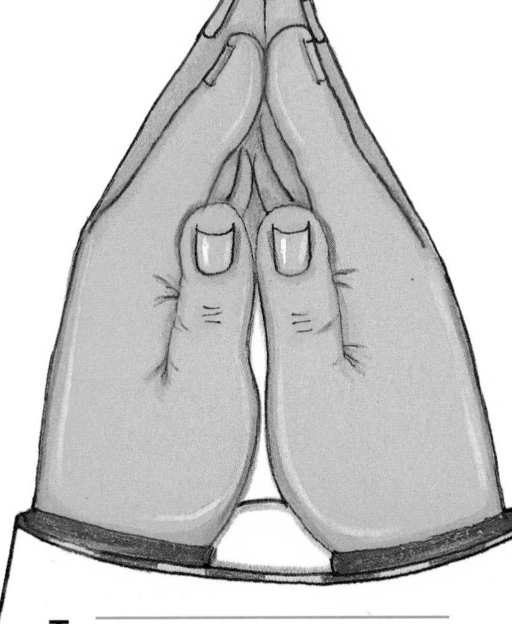

To ______________________

The Lord's Prayer.

Unit 3 Review

Write an X by the true sentences.

1. ______ Jesus teaches us about God.
2. ______ God does not care about us.
3. ______ God cares more about flowers than about people.
4. ______ We can always thank God.

Think about the story "Jesus Cares for a Sick Woman."

Talk about these questions.

1. How did Jesus show he cared for the woman?
2. How does Jesus show he cares for us?
3. What does Jesus want us to do for each other?

Unit 3 Review

Think about the story "The Good Samaritan."

Circle the correct answer.

1. Jesus teaches us to care for people. YES NO
2. The Samaritan helped the man who was robbed. YES NO
3. We should act like the leader of the people. YES NO
4. Only our parents can help people. YES NO

Circle the correct word to complete each sentence.

1. Jesus taught us The _____ Prayer.

   Lord's Brother's

2. "Hallowed" means _____.

   happy holy

3. "Trespass" means to _____.

   hurt someone help someone

LETTING OTHERS KNOW MY FEELINGS

How I choose to share my feelings can be hurtful to myself or others.

Activity

Is the feeling shared in a helpful or hurtful way?

Circle **OK** if the picture shows a helpful way to share feelings.

Circle **NOT OK** if the picture shows a way that is hurtful.

OK NOT OK

OK NOT OK

OK NOT OK

OK NOT OK

Draw a picture that shows you letting others know your feelings.

Following Jesus

Jesus loves me and calls me to be a loving person. One way I can show love is by sharing my feelings in a way that is helpful, not hurtful, to myself or others.

Growing Closer

IT IS IMPORTANT for every Christian to *know* The Lord's Prayer by heart. It is just as important to *understand* the meaning of the memorized words. Take some time with your family to talk about this common Christian prayer and what some of the phrases mean to each of you. As a family, try rewriting the prayer *in your own words.*

Prayer is one way we show our love and concern for others. "Please pray for me" is a special way of asking others to care for us. Perhaps your family has a special need for prayer at this time, or perhaps you are aware of another's need to be remembered in your prayer. Consider how your family can use prayer as a real way of expressing your caring concern for one another and for others.

Looking Ahead

In Unit 4, your child will be guided to experience belonging to the community of Jesus' friends. Few things are as important to a child's development as a Christian than to feel at home within a Christian community. Usually the child enters into this community through the Christian family. At Baptism the family and parish celebrate the entry of their new member. In this unit your child will learn about the sacrament of Baptism and recall his or her own experience of being welcomed into the community.

Opening Doors

A Take-Home Magazine™

A Closer Look

The Lord's Prayer

For those who continue to ask, "Lord, teach us to pray" (Luke 11:1), the prayer that Jesus taught his disciples is a worthwhile place to start.

It was seeing Jesus in prayer, in communion with his Father, that moved the disciples to ask how they also might pray. Jesus responded willingly to the disciples' request. When he taught the disciples to pray, Jesus used an ancient formula called a *kaddish.* Both he and the disciples would have been familiar with this form of prayer since childhood. The structure of the prayer includes:

- praise to God
- prayer for the coming of the kingdom
- petitions for God's blessings and forgiveness

Like a kaddish, prayed during the Jewish synagogue service, the Our Father is a community prayer. Catholics pray the Lord's Prayer each Sunday at Mass. It is in the spirit of unity that in many Catholic parishes, the community joins hands when praying the Lord's Prayer. When we pray this prayer, we are united not only with each other but also with Orthodox Christians, Protestants, Jews, and all those who proclaim God as Father and who pray for the coming of the kingdom.

The Peaceable Kingdom (Isaiah 11:6–7)

these dedicated religious baked the bricks needed to house the infirm themselves.

The Saint Vincent De Paul Society, a group of laymen who operate at the parish level, was first organized in America in 1845 to provide food, clothing, and fuel for the sick and the poor. The society also founded homes for destitute boys.

American Catholics responded to other social problems as well. In the 1870s the Industrial Revolution was in full gear, and the Christian Brothers responded by founding schools to teach boys industrial trade skills. Between 1870 and 1900, the Little Sisters of the Poor opened 34 homes for the aged, the Sisters of the Good Shepherd established homes for delinquent women, and the Sisters of Charity founded homes for abandoned infants and unwed mothers.

Since the early 1900s, Catholics have built and staffed many organizations to benefit the destitute. Today men and women of the Church have vowed to continue to be leaders of the social services as long as poverty and social inequity exists. As an example, Catholic Charities, a national organization, has set as its goals the elimination of the causes of poverty as well as the continued ministry to those in need. Religious orders are engaged in ever new and imaginative projects to help abused women, the aged, prisoners, and the homeless. Catholics continue to heed the words of Jesus: . . . "whatever you did for one of these least brothers of mine, you did for me" (Matthew 25:40).

Catholic Charitable Institutions in the 1990s	
Catholic hospitals	640
Dispensaries	206
Convalescent homes	667
Child welfare centers	239
Nurseries	496
Social service centers	1803
Saint Vincent De Paul societies	4700

A CARING CHURCH

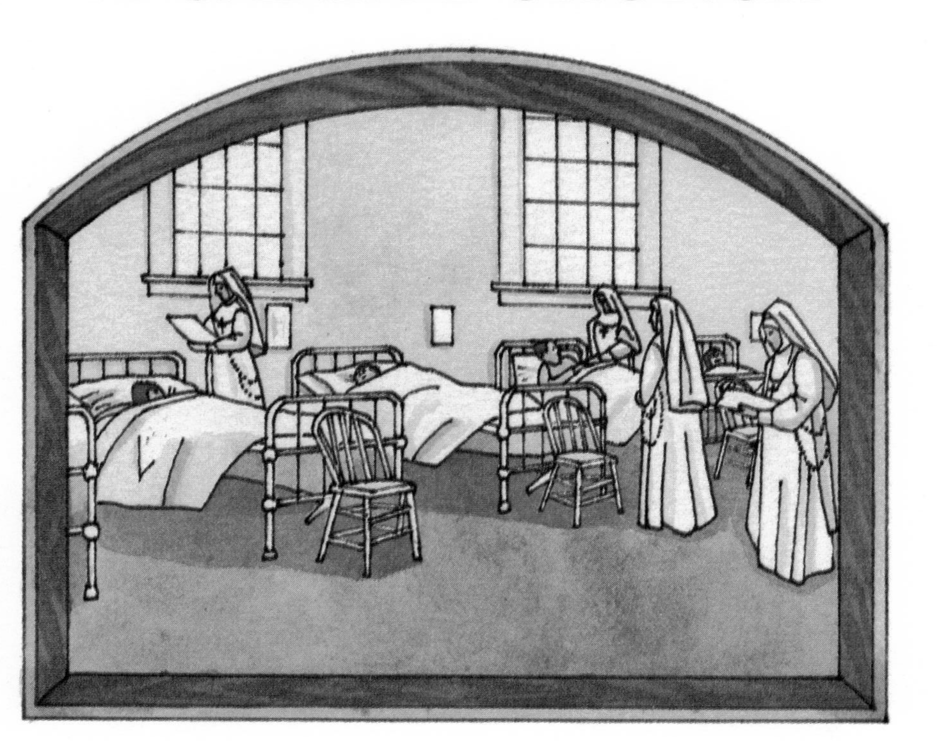

In religion class, your child is learning how God cares for us and how Jesus wants us to care for others. The Church is presented as people who try to care about others as Jesus did. American Catholics took this message to heart and dedicated themselves and their resources to works of mercy.

Catholic social action took hold in the late 1800s. Nursing for the poor was badly needed at the time of the great epidemics, and religious women and men (such as the Alexian Brothers, a community of male nurses) were among the first to meet the crisis. Many times

At Mass, we conclude the Lord's Prayer by saying,

> "For the kingdom, the power, and the glory are yours,
> now and forever."

Praying for the coming of the kingdom is an important petition in the Lord's Prayer. As Christians we believe that Jesus came to bring God's kingdom. Once Jesus was asked if he was the promised one who had come to establish the kingdom. He replied, "The blind regain their sight, the lame walk, lepers are cleansed, the deaf hear, the dead are raised, and the poor have the good news proclaimed to them" (Matthew 11:3-5). Jesus painted a word picture to affirm that he had come to bring about God's kingdom. It is a good image to keep in mind as we pray,

> "Thy kingdom come.
> thy will be done on earth as it is in heaven."

The prayer that Jesus taught us unites us with him in working to bring God's kingdom of love, peace, and justice to our world.

Give us this day our daily bread.

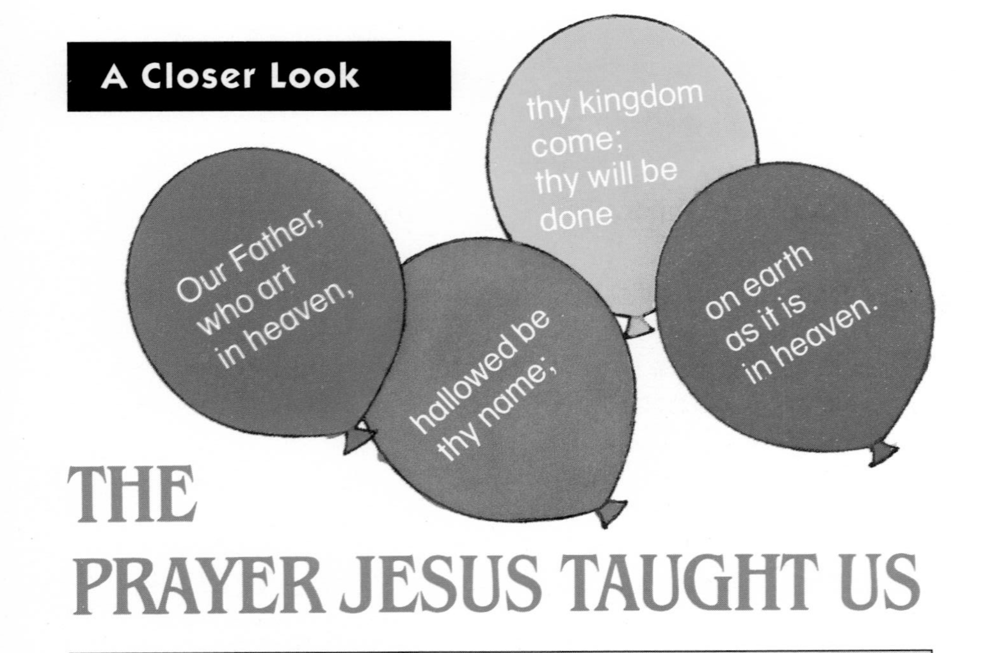

THE PRAYER JESUS TAUGHT US

The Lord's Prayer or Our Father is one prayer all Christians share. Help your child learn this important prayer of our faith by working through the activity on these pages, by praying it often at home, and by praying it with the Catholic Christian community gathered together at Mass.

At Mass I pray many prayers.
I pray prayers of thanks and praise.
I pray prayers of forgiveness.
I pray for God's help, too.

At Mass I pray the prayer Jesus taught us.
It is called The Lord's Prayer.
I can pray The Lord's Prayer everywhere!

Give us this day our daily bread;
and forgive us our trespasses
as we forgive those who trespass against us;
and lead us not into temptation,
but deliver us from evil.
Amen.

As your child learns each phrase, draw a string to the balloon. Decorate the ribbon when you have learned the whole prayer.

The next time you go to Mass, hold hands with the person next to you as you pray The Lord's Prayer.

UNIT 4

We Belong to the Catholic Church

Who makes you feel like you belong at home or at school?

We Are Christians

Sharing with Friends

It is good to have friends.
You tell stories to friends.
You tell friends how you feel.
You share with your friends.

Activity

What do you share with your friends?
Read the sentences below.
Then circle the sentences that tell
what you share with your friends.

I share toys with my friends.
I share food with my friends.
I share happy times with my friends.
I share what scares me with my friends.
I share secrets with my friends.

What are some things you do with your friends?

Jesus Our Friend

Jesus is our special friend.
We follow his example.
We care for others and try to
be a friend as Jesus showed us.

Another name for Jesus is **Christ**.
The friends of Jesus share this name.
We are called **Christians**.
We Christians are the friends and
followers of Jesus.

Trace over the letters
to complete the sentence.

I am a 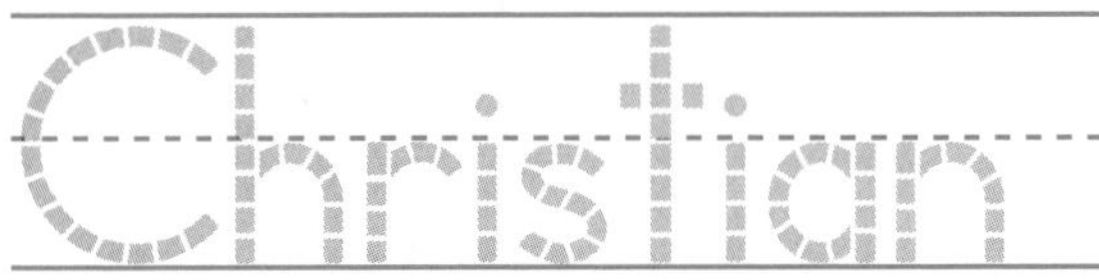

We Believe

We are the friends and followers of Jesus. We call ourselves Christians.

New Words

Christ The name Christ means that "Jesus was sent by God to help all people."

Christian A Christian is a friend and follower of Jesus Christ.

Making Friends with Jesus

One afternoon Andrew saw Jesus walking down the road to town. Andrew wanted to be Jesus' friend, so he hurried to catch up with Jesus.

Behind him, Jesus heard Andrew's footsteps. He stopped, looked around, and saw Andrew. "What are you looking for?" Jesus asked.

Because Andrew wanted to get to know Jesus better, he asked, "Where are you staying?"

"Come and you will see," Jesus said.

Jesus and Andrew walked to Jesus' home.
They spent the rest of the day together.
They liked one another a lot.
Jesus and Andrew became good friends.

Based on John 1: 35–39

Activity

Jesus is Andrew's friend,
and Jesus is my friend, too.
This is one way Jesus is my friend.

Love One Another

Besides Andrew, Jesus had other friends.
Peter, Andrew's brother, was
a friend of Jesus, too.
Some of his other friends were Mary,
Martha, and Lazarus, their brother.
They liked Jesus to come to their house.

Jesus told all his friends something
important, "If you are my friends,
you will love one another."

Based on John 13:35

The friends of Jesus did try to love one another.

They gave their clothes to keep people warm.

They cooked bread for hungry people.

They helped sick people get better.

They shared their money with poor people.

Activity

There is a symbol in front of each sentence above. Draw the symbol in the box by the picture that matches the sentence.

Acting like Friends

When there's playing
To be done,
I need a friend
To make it fun.

When there's work
I have to do,
It's always easy
When there's two.

Laughing, sharing
All life brings,
I need a friend
For all these things.

Give names to the children in the pictures
who are acting like friends.
Tell stories about them.

Acting like Jesus

We Christians are the friends and followers of Jesus.
Here are some things Christians do.

▲ We use the cross as a sign of Jesus' love for us.

▼ We care about the world.

▲ We care especially about people.

▲ We respect and read the Bible.

◀ We pray The Lord's Prayer.

Praying for Others

Jesus prays for everyone because he loves us all.
As the friends and followers of Jesus,
we can pray for others, too.

We can pray for

- sick people,
- hungry people,
- poor people,
- people who need clothing.

Activity

Draw a picture of the people you will pray for today.

Chapter Review

Choose a word to complete each sentence.

Christians l________ one another.

Christians h________ others.

Christians s________ with people.

Christians p________.

1. What name do Jesus' friends and followers call themselves?

2. What is another name for Jesus?

3. Talk about what we can do to show that we are Jesus' friends and followers.

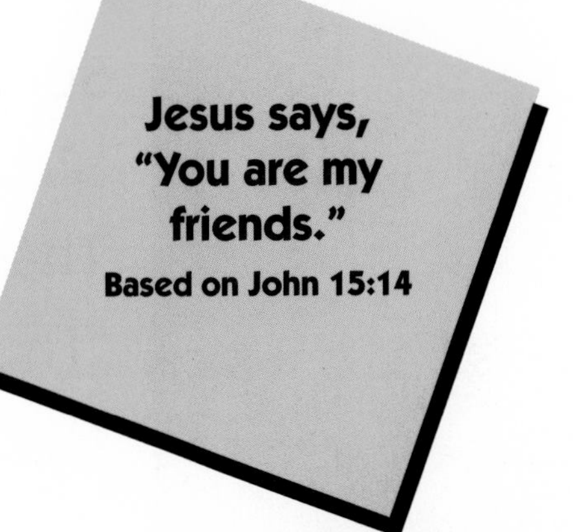

We Welcome New Christians at Baptism

How does your family celebrate birthdays?

Celebrating Being Alive

Birthdays celebrate our being alive.
Our families and friends are glad we are alive and belong to them.

Sometimes our family and friends give birthday parties for us.
They are saying, "You are special."
"Thank God you are in our family."
"Thank God you are our friend."

A Member of the Family of Jesus

Baptism is a sacrament.
A **sacrament** is a celebration of Jesus' love and God's presence.
Baptism celebrates our new life with Jesus.

We live our new life with all other Christians.
Through **Baptism**, they become our brothers and sisters.
Together we are the family of Jesus.

Jesus said to his followers, "Baptize all people in the name of the Father, and of the Son, and of the Holy Spirit."

Based on Matthew 28:19

We Believe

At Baptism we celebrate becoming a member of the family of Jesus. We celebrate our new life as brothers and sisters of Jesus.

New Words

sacrament A sacrament is a celebration of Jesus' love and of God's presence.

Baptism Baptism is a celebration of our new life with Jesus and his friends.

Rosa's Baptism

1. Father Alberto and other members of San Jose Church welcome Rosa. Father Alberto and Rosa's parents and **godparents** make the Sign of the Cross on Rosa's forehead.

2. Father Alberto reads a story about Jesus from the Bible. Everyone prays for little Rosa. They promise to help Rosa know, love, and trust God.

3. Father Alberto pours water over Rosa's head three times. He says, "I baptize you, Rosa, in the name of the Father, and of the Son, and of the Holy Spirit."

4. Father Alberto marks Rosa's head with blessed oil.

5. Rosa receives a white robe. Father Alberto prays that she will grow to be like Jesus.

6. Rosa's father lights a candle from the Easter candle. It reminds everyone of Jesus, the Light of the World.
7. The members of San Jose Church stand and clap to welcome Rosa into the family of Jesus.

Activity

On the lines below, write your godparents' names. They help you live as a friend of Jesus.

New Word

godparents Godparents are people who help us grow as friends and followers of Jesus.

Activity

Many things can be signs that we are celebrating a birthday.
Circle the things that are usually part of your birthday celebration.

   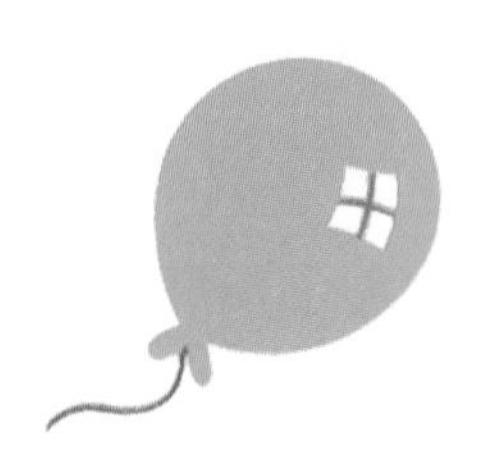

Special Signs of Baptism

Catholics use many signs to celebrate the sacrament of Baptism.

Here is what happened at your Baptism.

There was a reading from the 

.

The priest poured  on your head.

The priest marked your head with 

.

You were dressed in a white  .

Your parents lighted a 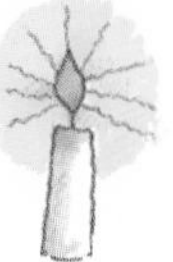 from the Easter 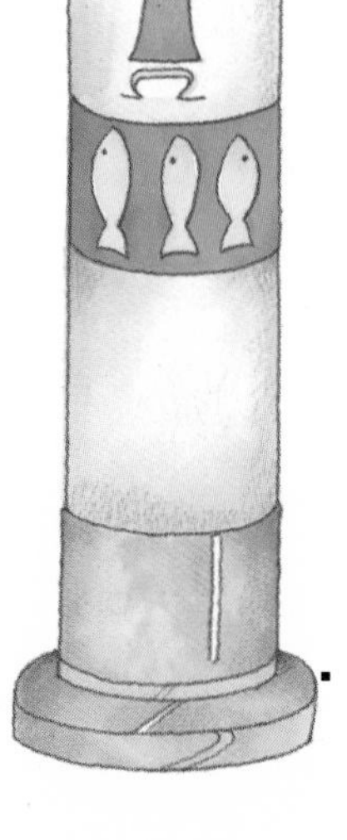

.

Finish this picture.

Make it a picture of yourself.

My Christian name is

____

____.

Activity

It is good to think about our own Baptism.
Draw what you imagine your Baptism was like.

Holy Water

We can make the Sign of the Cross with holy water. It reminds us that the priest poured water over our heads at Baptism. It reminds us of our new life with Jesus.

Celebrating Baptism

The sacrament of Baptism celebrates our becoming friends with Jesus. We remember our Christian family.

We are baptized.

We become Christians.

The followers of Jesus welcome us.

God is our Father.

Jesus is our brother.

We are all brothers and sisters.

Mary

Praying a Litany

At Baptism the priest asks our parents,
"What name do you give this child?"
Then our parents tell the priest our name.
They almost always give us a saint's name.

Joseph

Saints are people who love God very much.
They spend their lives doing good things for others.
Now they live with God in heaven.
They can ask God to help us.

Peter

Here is a way to ask the saints to help us.
This kind of prayer is called a litany.

Andrew

Lazarus

Leader: Mother Mary,
All: Pray to God for us.
Leader: Saint Joseph,
All: Pray to God for us.
Leader: Peter and Andrew,
All: Pray to God for us.
Leader: Martha, Mary,
and Lazarus,
All: Pray to God for us.

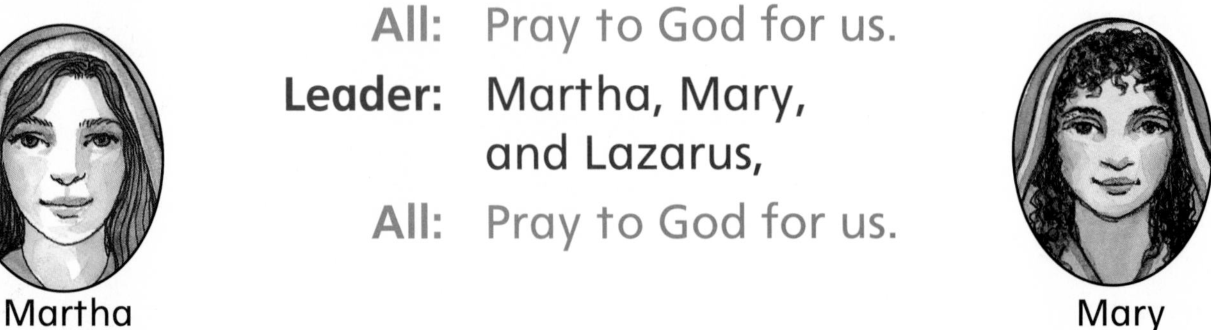

Martha

Mary

Chapter Review

Activity

Circle what you can see at Baptism.

1. Whose family do we join at Baptism?

2. What do we call the celebration of becoming a member of the family of Jesus?

3. Talk about what it means to be in the family of Jesus.

Love each other like brothers and sisters.
Based on Romans 12:10

15

We Are Catholics

Name some places where you feel that you belong.

My Home

Inside my home
Lives a family
Of people who
Belong to me.

Inside my home
We laugh and play,
Eat and help,
And read and pray.

Inside my home
We're taught to share
And care for people
everywhere.

▼ Holy Assumption Russian Orthodox Church, Kenai, Alaska

▲ Solvang Catholic Mission, Santa Ynez Valley, California

Where We Belong

We belong to our families.
As friends and followers
of Jesus, we also belong
to his Christian family.
We gather in groups called
Churches.
The Church we belong to is
called the **Catholic Church.**

▲ St. Paul's Episcopal Church, Port Townsend, Washington

We Believe

Christians gather in groups called Churches. We belong to the Catholic Church.

New Words

Church	We belong to the Catholic Church.

Allie's Family Shares Love

Allie's mother helps her get ready for school. Her mother helps her be happy in the Johnson family.

Allie and her father walk the dog each evening. Then Allie enjoys belonging to the Johnsons.

Her brother Johnny tells her jokes on the way to school. When they laugh, she loves belonging to her family.

Write something your family members do to let you know that they love you.

____

____

Belonging to Our Catholic Family

At Sunday Mass, the Johnson family says hello to Father Mike. The Johnsons know many of the other people at Mass, too. Knowing so many people helps Allie's family feel they belong to Saint John Church.

Allie's mom helps pack bags of baby clothes for mothers who need them. Allie comes along to help pack. She puts a teddy bear in each bag. Allie likes to help others. It is fun to pack bags with the grown-ups and other children. It helps make her feel that she belongs to Saint John Church.

In Our Catholic Church

Here is another meaning of the word church.
A **church** is a special place where Christians come together to pray.

Allie and the her family go to Saint John Catholic Church. They see and hear many things.

Allie genuflects.

Soon a boy or a girl lights the candles.

The organ fills the church with music.

Then the priest, the servers, and the reader walk down the aisle. All the people stand and sing.

The reader puts the book with the Bible stories on the lectern.

The priest bows before the altar. He kisses it.

With the priest, the people make the Sign of the Cross.

Activity

Put an **X** by all the things you see in your church.
Then talk about other things you see at church.

New Word

church A church is a special place where Christians come together to pray.

Activity

Catholics, like other Christians, are called by God to love Jesus and all other people. Here are some things Catholics do.

Circle the number in each set of sentences that tells what is happening in the picture.

1. Followers of Jesus feed the hungry.
2. Followers of Jesus visit the sick.
3. Followers of Jesus study the Bible.

1. Catholics help to buy a van to pick up people who cannot drive anymore.
2. Catholics have a square dance to help everyone become better friends.
3. Some Catholics teach in the Catholic school.

1. Some Catholics take Holy Communion to people who cannot get to Mass.
2. Some of the family of Jesus sing in the choir.
3. Men and women read from the book of Bible stories at church.

Activity

The name of our parish is

____

____.

Praying With Jesus

One day Jesus said something very important to his friends and followers. "Where people come together in my name, I am there with them," he told them.

Based on Matthew 18:20

What did Jesus mean?
When we gather with other Catholics, Jesus is with us.
We belong to the Church, the family of Jesus.
We pray with Jesus to God the Father.

Chapter Review

Activity

You belong to the Catholic Church.
Circle all the things you see in church.

1. To which Christian Church do we belong?

2. What word means both a group of Christians and the place where they gather?

3. Talk about what you like best about your church.

Jesus says, "Where people come together in my name, I am there with them."
Based on Matthew 18:20

16

We Come Together for Mass

What is the best thing that happens when your family gathers together to eat a meal?

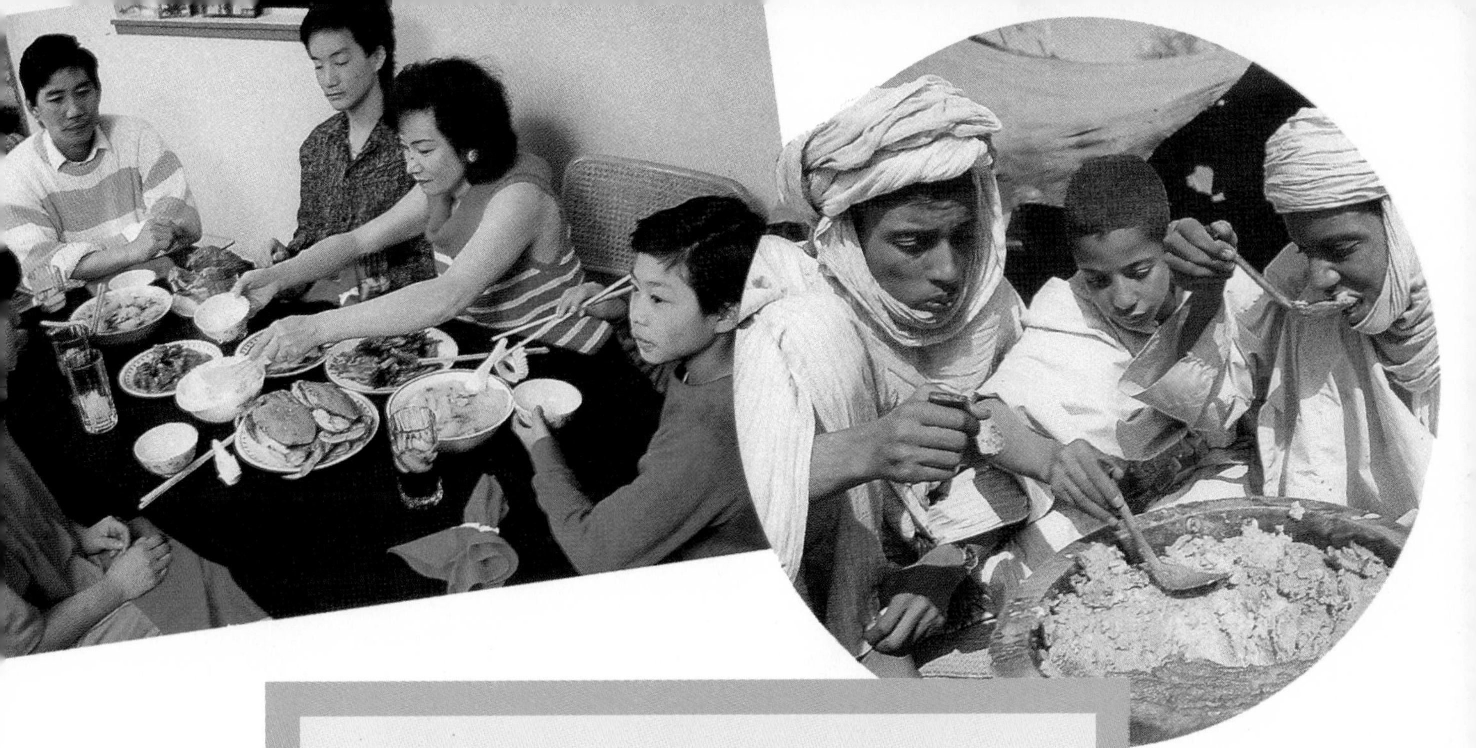

Catholics Celebrate the Mass

Families share meals together.
The Catholic family shares a meal, too.
We call this meal the **Mass** or the **Eucharist.**
Jesus shares this special meal with us.

New Words

Mass	The Mass is a special meal Jesus shares with us.
Eucharist	The Eucharist is another name for the Mass.

A Meal with Jesus

One evening Jesus shared a
very special meal with his friends.

Jesus picked up some bread.
He thanked God and broke the
bread into pieces.
Jesus said, "This is my body.
Take this, all of you, and eat it."

Activity

What did Jesus tell his friends to do?
Trace Jesus' words.

Do this to
remember me.

We Believe

The Mass is a special meal with Jesus. Jesus gives himself to us at Mass.

Remembering Special Words

When Salvatore thinks of Grandma, he remembers her stories and hugs.
He also remembers the special words she said to him when she was cooking.

"What a big boy you are!"
"What a good reader you are!"
"What a fast ball player you are!"
"I love you!"

Activity

Write some wonderful words you remember special people saying to you.

____

____.

Remembering Jesus' Words

At Mass, God speaks to us through
the words of the Bible.
We listen to the reader read
God's word of love.

The priest says, "The Lord be with you."
We answer, "And also with you."

Then the priest reads a story of Jesus.
The story tells us about how much
Jesus loves and cares for us.
We can love him back in our daily life.

Activity

Trace the words that tell you
Jesus is always with us.

The Lord be

Remembering Grandma

Salvatore misses Grandma who
moved away last year.
But he remembers her hugs,
her stories, and her cooking.

Then something happened.
Grandma got on a plane.
She came to visit Salvatore.

Salvatore's father took
him to the airport to
pick up Grandma.
As she hugged
Salvatore, she
said, "I will
cook all your
favorite foods."

That night Grandma
cooked spaghetti for supper.
"This is better than any spaghetti I
remember," he said.
"But Grandma, do you know what the
best part of this meal is?
You are with us!"

Remembering Jesus

The Mass is our special meal with Jesus.
We remember what he said and did at
the special meal he ate with his friends.
The priest does what Jesus did.
The priest says what Jesus said.
“This is my body.
This is my blood,”
says Father Williams.

At Mass, Jesus gives us the Bread of Life.
With this bread we remember Jesus.
When we eat this bread, Jesus is with us.
As friends of Jesus, we share in Jesus’ life.

Praying Amen

At Mass we pray with Jesus.
With him, we say "Amen."

Amen means "Yes!"
"Yes, God, I love you."
"Yes, God, I trust you."
"Yes, God, I want to help
you care for the world."
"Yes, God, I thank you for
your love."

Activity

Color the letters to show how you feel when you pray "Amen" at Mass.

Chapter Review

Activity

Circle the words that are about the Mass.

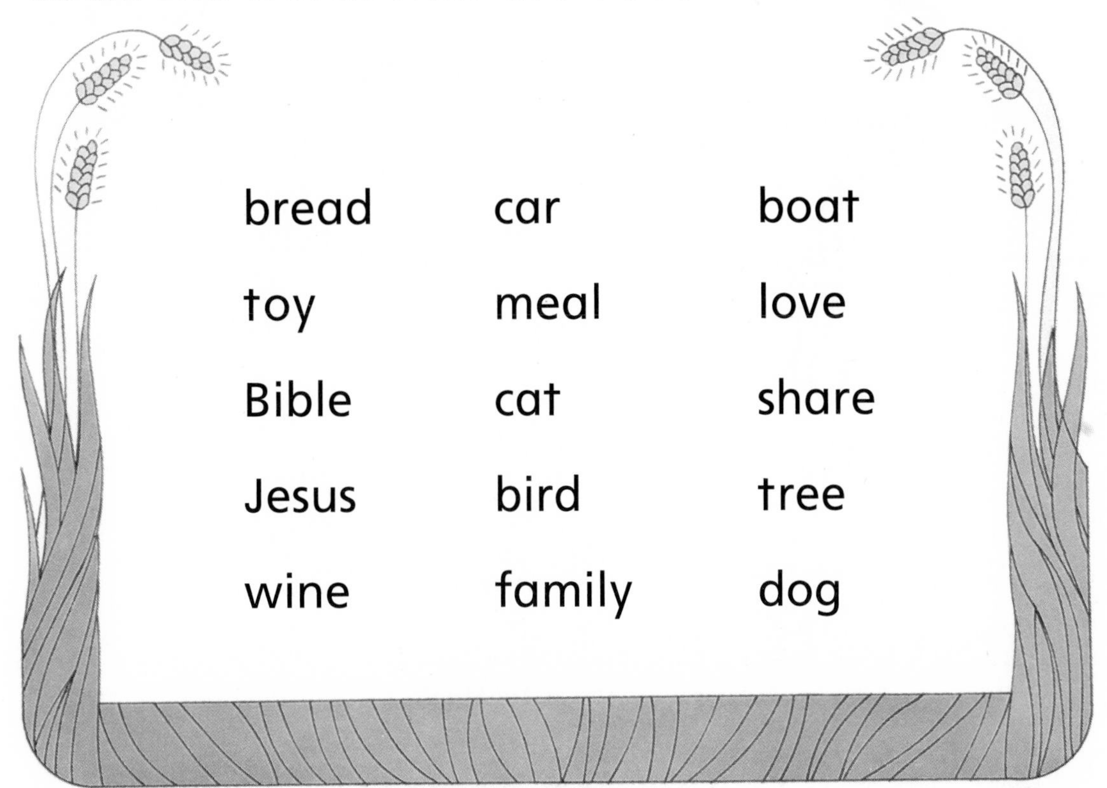

1. What do we call the special meal Jesus shares with us?

____

2. Who gives himself to us at Mass?

____

3. Talk about what you hear, see, and do at Mass.

Jesus says, "I am the Bread of Life."
Based on John 6:35

UNIT 4 ORGANIZER

Fill in the blanks.

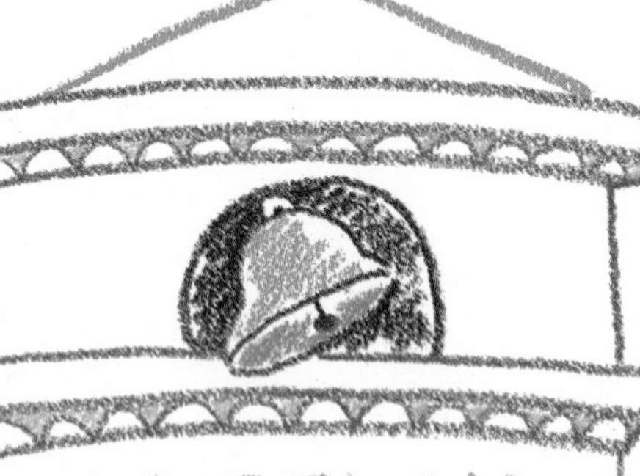

WE BELONG TO THE

____

CHURCH

WE WELCOME NEW CHRISTIANS

AT ________________

WE COME TOGETHER

FOR ________________

Review

Circle the correct answer.

1. We are Catholic Christians. Yes No
2. The word church has one meaning. Yes No
3. Our church has an altar. Yes No
4. Jesus is with us as the Bread of Life. Yes No

Circle the word that best completes the sentence.

1. At __________ we become part of Jesus' family.
   Mass Baptism
2. The word Church means a group of __________.
   Christians homes
3. The word church also means a special __________.
   person place
4. Jesus shares a special meal with us at __________.
   Mass Baptism

Unit 4 Review

Fill in the first letter of each picture.

1. _____ ar
2. _____ pple
3. _____ ent
4. _____ at
5. _____ wl
6. _____ ine
7. _____ ce
8. _____ ar

The first letters form a new word.

Write the new word to finish the message.

Our Church home is the __________ Church.

TELLING OTHERS HOW I FEEL

Boots and Zip
share toys.
They share
fun times playing.
Boots and Zip
share feelings.

Activity

Pretend you are Boots and use "I-feel talk."
Tell how you feel about sharing with Zip.

I feel ____________ when ____________
____
______________________________.

Activity

Circle the feeling that you would most like to have!

Happy Sad Mad Proud Surprised

A Prayer

Jesus, I feel happy when my mom gives me a hug.
I feel sad when others won't let me play.
I feel joy when I help a friend.
I feel peaceful when you are near.

Growing Closer

THINK ABOUT MASS in your parish. As a family, consider the questions below.

Which of the Masses in your parish is your favorite?
What is your favorite gospel story?
What is your favorite song or hymn?
What is your favorite part of the Mass?
If you could change one thing about the Mass, what would it be?

TO FEEL WELCOME is a need we all understand. With your family, discuss how you as a Catholic family welcome friends, family members, and strangers to your home. Talk about ways your family may consider improving the hospitality already present in your home.

Looking Ahead

In Unit 5 your child will learn that Jesus promised to send his followers the Holy Spirit as a helper and guide. The Spirit would be with them, helping them to be united as brothers and sisters. The Spirit would strengthen them, helping them live caring, just, peaceful, and happy lives. Jesus fulfilled his promise of sending his Spirit after his death and resurrection. That same Spirit is still at work in our hearts and in our communities.

OPENING DOORS

A Take-Home Magazine™

THE MASS BEGINS

They assemble: young men and women, first time parents sharing the care of the baby; the nuns who serve the parish; the elderly who walk perkily up to the front pews, obviously comfortable in their environs; and the young who cluster in bunches with their friends. This is the Christian community gathering for Sunday Mass.

The importance of this assembled group cannot be overestimated. They are the community of Jesus' followers and he is present with them. "For where two or three are gathered together in my name, there am I in the midst of them," Jesus said (Matthew 18:20).

Dutch and Belgian families gather around bonfires on Holy Saturday night, set off firecrackers, and ring bells. Children believe the joyful sound of the bells brings their colorful Easter eggs.

Hungarians paint their Easter eggs red to commemorate Christ's blood shed on Good Friday. Throughout Hungary, ruby-colored shells hanging from the branches of Easter trees can be seen.

Austrians bake special yeast breads for Easter. *Österstollen*, a raisin, braided bread and *Butterküchen*, dotted with butter, sugar, and cinnamon, are favorites.

What foods and customs do you enjoy at Easter? Perhaps, you would like to revive some of your family's ethnic traditions.

Each Easter season, magazines beguile us with glossy pages of artistically decorated eggs, ethnic recipes, and native folk costumes. These are the traditions and customs of our immigrant ancestors that continue to intrigue so many of us. A few such customs are listed below.

EASTER TRADITIONS

Swedish children write Easter letters to say *Glad Pask*, which means "Happy Easter." Of course, their delightful childish drawings add to the charm of the cards. On the night before Easter, they drop these greeting cards off at the homes of their friends and relatives. This night routinely ends with fireworks to light the night, reminiscent of the bright light of the resurrection.

Polish families make table centerpieces consisting of a sugared lamb resting on green leaves. Around the lamb are dishes of cold roast pork, sausage, salads, sweetmeats, and brightly colored hard-boiled eggs, called *pisanki.* According to legend, when Mary Magdalene went to the tomb of Jesus, she took some hard-boiled eggs to eat. When she saw the risen Christ, the eggs were miraculously painted in rainbow colors.

Irish families enjoy sunrise services on Easter morning. For breakfast, they feast on eggs and "golden bread," which is similar to French toast. Many communities hold dance competitions on Easter Sunday as an occasion for the townsfolk to spend the day together, certainly appropriate for the community of Jesus.

The presence of Jesus in the eucharistic celebration is discussed by the bishops in the documents of the Second Vatican Council. There they reiterate the reality of Jesus' presence under the appearance of the bread and wine and emphasize his presence when the Scripture readings are proclaimed. Furthermore, the bishops clearly state that Jesus is present with his gathered community at Mass.

As the Mass begins, the community of Jesus stands and sings the gathering song. Giving us a common focus, this song merges our individual thoughts and feelings as we prepare to celebrate our common faith. The song also sets the theme for the Mass. If the tone of the Mass is one of jubilation, the gathering hymn is jubilant, too; if the character of the celebration is more reflective, the song expresses this mood.

Then the priest greets us with these words:

> "The grace of our Lord Jesus Christ and the love of God
> and the fellowship of the Holy Spirit be with you all."

These words remind us that we begin the Mass with the Holy Trinity active within the community of Jesus.

Aware that we are in God's presence, we become more and more conscious of our faults. Thus we pause to admit our sinfulness and rely on God's mercy.

Confident of God's forgiveness, our hearts are ready to praise God in the beautiful hymn of the *Gloria.*

> Lord God, heavenly King,
> almighty God and Father,
> we worship you, we give you thanks,
> we praise you for your glory.

With these sentiments of praise and thanksgiving in our hearts, the community joins with the priest as he prays the Opening Prayer, and the Mass begins. We are open to hear the word of the "Holy One, the Most High Jesus Christ," in the Scriptures, and we are ready to celebrate the Eucharist.

Catholics Gather

Your child has probably experienced Sunday Mass. Now discover together the significance of the Gathering Rite that brings us together as members of one family and prepares us to celebrate the Liturgy of the Word and the Liturgy of the Eucharist. Then help your child complete the activity that follows.

Read Along

I go to Mass on Sunday. At Mass I celebrate belonging to the family of Jesus.

Sometimes people at the church door welcome my family. They welcome other families, too.

When the Mass begins, the song leader helps me to sing a happy song. I remember that Jesus is with us. I remember that we belong to him and to each other.

Now I am ready to listen to stories from the Bible. Now I am ready to celebrate Jesus in the Eucharist.

Unscramble the letters. You will discover something important about going to Mass!

suseJ si ihwt su ta sasM

____

____

The next time you go to Mass remember to thank Jesus for making you a member of his special family.

UNIT 5

The Holy Spirit Helps Us

Jesus Gives Us the Holy Spirit

Feeling Alone

Sometimes people feel alone.
They need the gift of friendship.

We Are Not Alone

Jesus did not want his friends to feel lonely.
Jesus did not leave his friends alone.
He does not leave us alone.
Jesus gives us the **Holy Spirit**.

What are some things you need to be happy?

The Gift from Jesus

The Holy Spirit is God, who is always with us to help us. One of the most important things we need is help to live like Jesus.

The Holy Spirit helps us live like Jesus.
The Holy Spirit helps us be strong and brave, happy and joyful as Jesus was.
The Holy Spirit helps us forgive others and be at peace as Jesus was.

Activity

Draw a picture of something good Jesus did.

We Believe

The Holy Spirit is God. Jesus gives us the Holy Spirit to be with us and to help us.

New Word

Holy Spirit The Holy Spirit is God.

The Gift of the Holy Spirit

Jesus' friends were sad and afraid.
They were sad because Jesus died.
They were afraid because they thought they were in danger, too.
They felt alone without Jesus.

Suddenly, Jesus was with them.
"Peace be with you," he said.
Jesus' friends were happy to see him.
Jesus had come to give them a gift.
He said, "Receive the Holy Spirit."

Jesus' friends felt comforted.
They felt less afraid.
The Holy Spirit was with them.

Based on John 19:22

Activity

Underline the words Jesus said in the story.
Copy the words below.

The Holy Spirit, Our Helper

When we are baptized, people
give us gifts.
They give us crosses, medals, and
other things.

At our Baptism, Jesus
gives us a gift, too.
Jesus gives us the Holy
Spirit.

Jesus gives us the Holy Spirit
to be our helper.
What does the Holy Spirit
help us to do?

Based on Galatians 5:22

The Holy Spirit Is Always with Us!

At Baptism we receive the Holy Spirit.
We can trust the Holy Spirit to be with us
and to help us.

We are children
Who are happy.
We are children
Who are sad.

Sometimes we may
Choose good things.
Sometimes we may
Choose bad.

But wherever
There are children,
God is watching
Lovingly.

In God's Spirit
We are strengthened.
In God's Spirit
We are free.

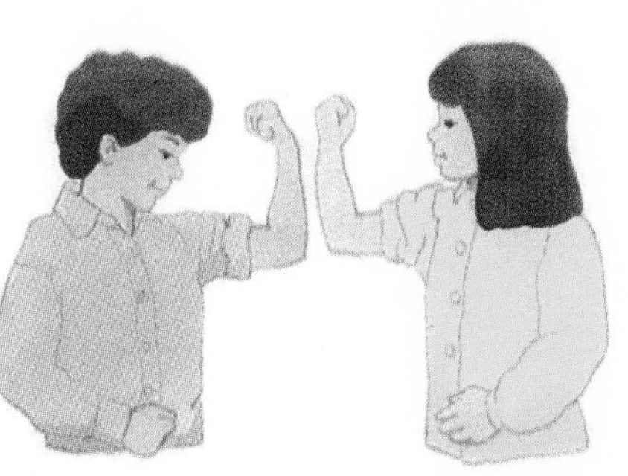

To Live Like Jesus

We want to live as
Jesus showed us.
How did Jesus act?
Jesus was very brave
and kind.
He was peaceful
and forgiving.
He was full of joy.
He was a friend
to everyone.
Who will help us
act like Jesus?

Activity

Write a prayer to ask the Holy Spirit
to help you act like Jesus.

Dear Holy Spirit,

Activity

Who acted like Jesus to help each person?
Look at the pictures on the left.
Match them with a picture on the right.
Write the correct letter in each box.

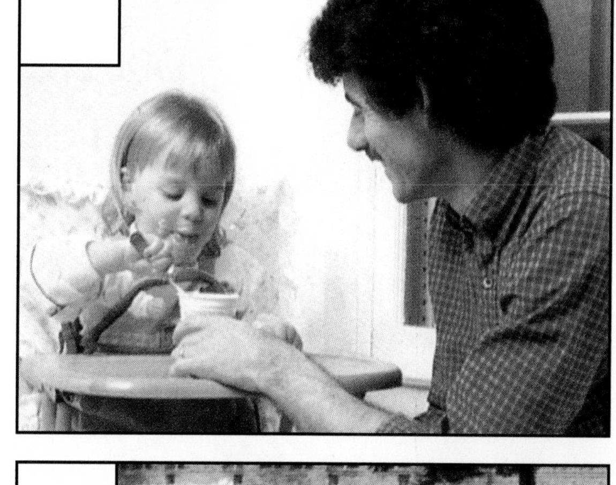

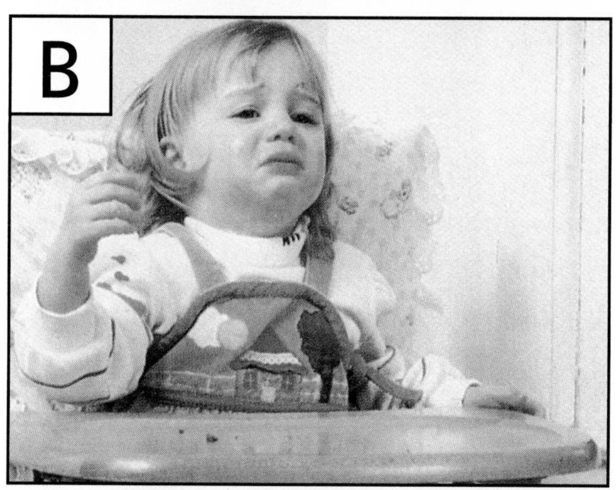

Praying to the Holy Spirit

We can pray to God the Holy Spirit.

Make a banner like the one here.

Print the name of an action you want the Holy Spirit to help you with.

Decorate your banner.

Chapter Review

The Holy Spirit helps us to act like Jesus.
Circle the ways you can act like Jesus.

1. Whom did Jesus give his friends to help them?

2. Why does Jesus give us the Holy Spirit?

3. Talk about ways in which the Holy Spirit helps you act like Jesus.

Jesus says, "The Holy Spirit is with you."
Based on John 14:16–17

18

The Holy Spirit Gives Us Strength

Sometimes We're Afraid

Tell about a time when you were afraid. What frightened you?

Mike had a scary dream.

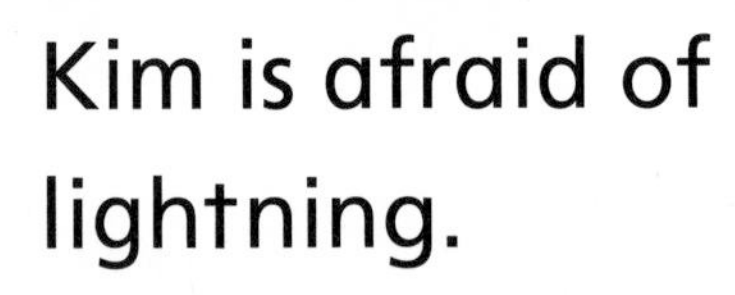

Kim is afraid of lightning.

Ruth is afraid of the dark.

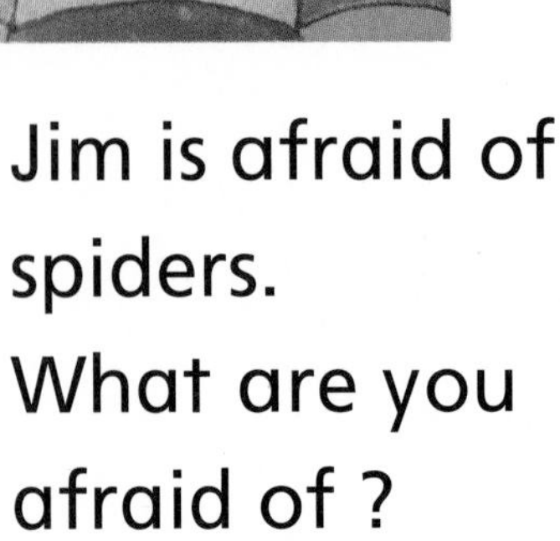

Jim is afraid of spiders.
What are you afraid of ?

Activity

Draw a picture in the space of someone helping you when you are afraid.

Come, Holy Spirit, Help Us

Jesus helps us when we are afraid. He gives us the Holy Spirit to help us be brave.

When we are afraid, we can pray, "Come, Holy Spirit, help us be brave."

We Believe

Jesus helps us when we are afraid. He gives us the Holy Spirit to help us be brave.

A Terrible Storm

One day Jesus and his friends were
in a fishing boat.
A storm came up suddenly.
Jesus was asleep.
The wind whistled and whipped up
the waves.
Water splashed into the boat.
The boat began to sink.

"Jesus, help us!" shouted his friends.
"We will all drown!"

Jesus woke up.
"Why are you so afraid?" he asked.
"I am with you."

Jesus stood up in the boat.
He faced the wind and the waves.
"Be still!" Jesus shouted. "Be calm!"
The wind and the waves became
calm and still.
Jesus' friends were no longer afraid.
They were glad Jesus was with them.

Based on Luke 8:22–25

This is a story from the **Gospel** of Luke.
The gospel is the good news of Jesus
found in the Bible.

Activity

What is the good news of Jesus?
Find the words and circle them.

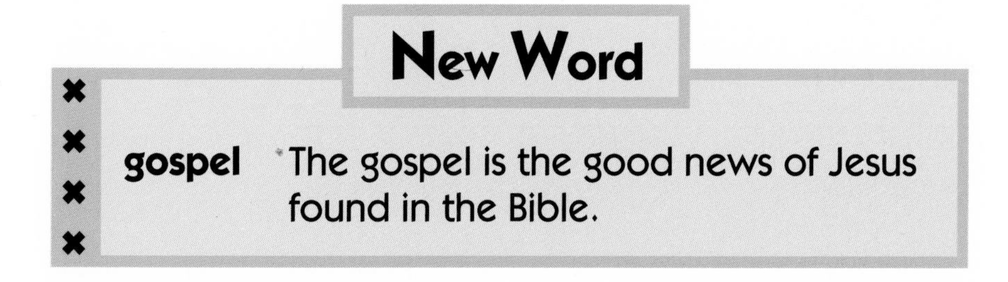

Help When We Are Scared

Timothy had a test to take.
He had to spell ten words.
He was worried.
Who could help him?

Bena had to act in a play.
She had to remember
all the words.
She was nervous.
Who could help her?

Kim had a bad fever.
He had to get a flu shot.
He was scared.
Who could help him?

Activity

What makes you worry?
Who gives you strength
when you are afraid?

The Holy Spirit Helps Us

Jesus gives us the Holy Spirit to help us when we are afraid. Sometimes the Holy Spirit helps us by giving us people who take care of us.

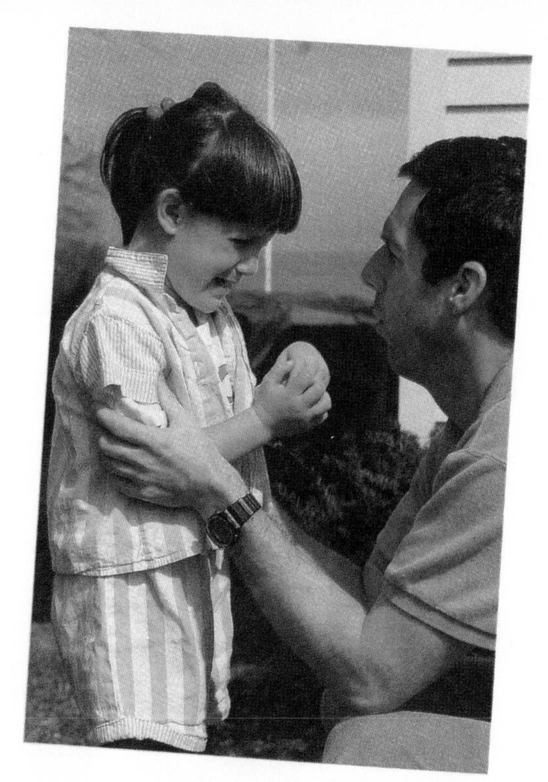

Activity

Put the words in order to find the good news. Write it in a sentence.

Activity

Look at these pictures.
Some of the people are afraid.
They ask the Holy Spirit to help them.
Whom has the Holy Spirit sent to help?

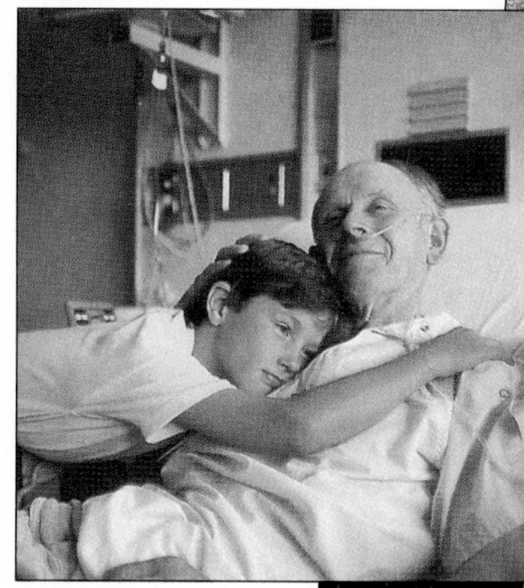

Come, Spirit of Love

God wants us to help people who are afraid.
The Holy Spirit helps us use our minds and hearts to help others.

Activity

Think about how you can help someone to be brave.
Whom will you help?

____

____

What will you do?

____

____

Praying with a Poster

We can hang up posters to remind us of God the Holy Spirit.
Decorate the poster below.

Chapter Review

Cross out all the G letters to find the message.

Copy the message below.

G	G	G	C	O	M	E	G	G	G	H	O	L	Y	G	G	G	S	P	I	R	I	T	G	G	G
G	G	H	E	L	P	G	G	M	E	G	G	G	G	B	E	G	G	G	B	R	A	V	E	G	G

1. How does Jesus help us when we are afraid?

2. What do we call the good news of Jesus?

3. Talk about ways the Holy Spirit helps you to be brave and strong.

Jesus says, "Do not be afraid. I will send you the Holy Spirit."
Based on John 14:16–18

The Holy Spirit Gives Us Peace

My friend told me I could not win
When I thought I could.
So then I did not try as hard
As I usually would.

I told her I was mad at her,
And then I walked away.
But now I'm feeling very sad.
I miss her when I play.

Sometimes we hurt each other,
Not really meaning to.
But we can always make things right
By the kind things that we do.

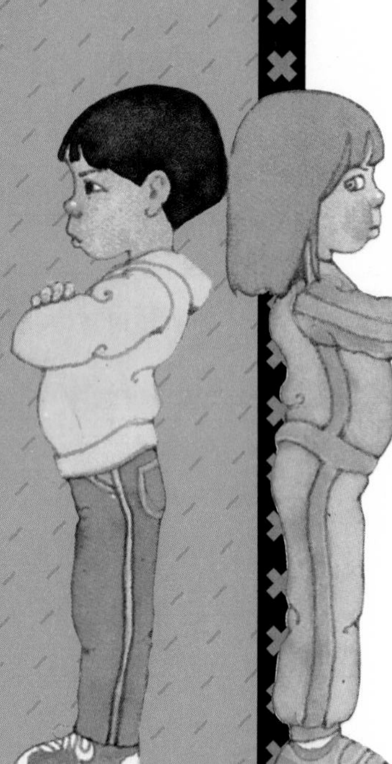

What are some ways to make up and be at peace after hurting someone or being hurt?

God Forgives Us

God always wants to forgive us.

God's **forgiveness** brings us peace and happiness.

Jesus brings us God's forgiveness.

Activity

Jesus gives us the Spirit of peace.

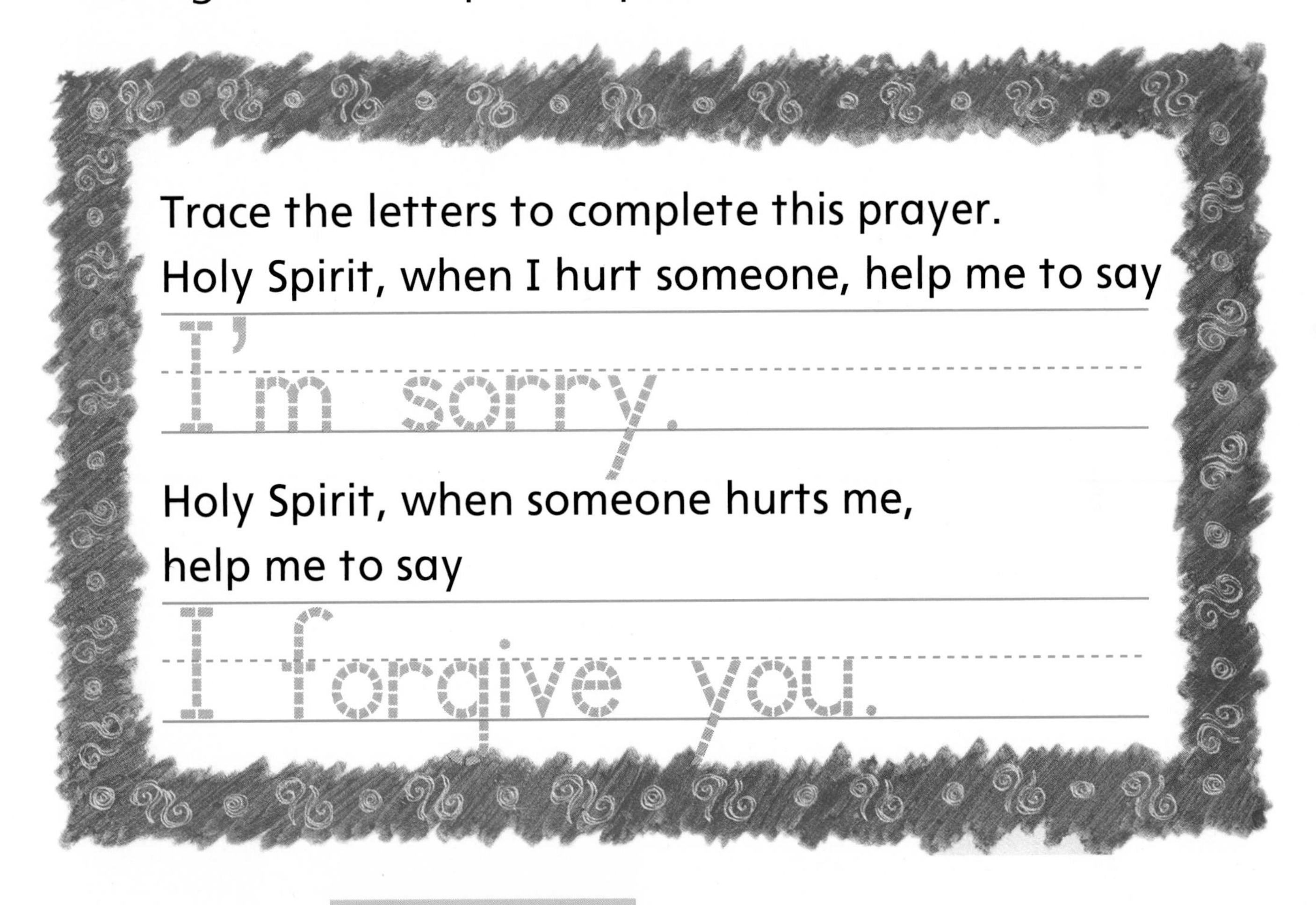

New Word

forgiveness Forgiveness means excusing or pardoning someone.

Jesus Forgives

A man named Zacchaeus loved
money more than people.
He cheated others to become rich.
But Zacchaeus was not happy.

One day Jesus came to town.
Zacchaeus wanted to see Jesus.
But Zacchaeus was too short to
see over the people's heads.
So he climbed a tree.

When Jesus saw the man
up in the tall tree, Jesus said,
"Come down, Zacchaeus.
Take me to your house."

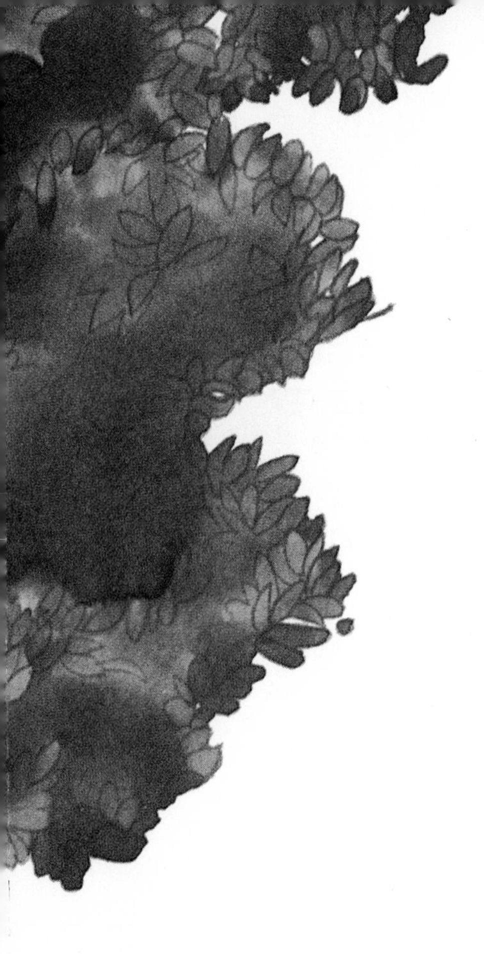

This made some people angry
because they thought Zacchaeus
did bad things.
But Jesus was kind to Zacchaeus.

"I'll pay back all the money I took
from people," Zacchaeus told Jesus.
"I am very sorry."
"God's forgiveness has come
to you, Zacchaeus," Jesus said.
"Be at peace."

Based on Luke 19:1–10

Activity

1. Zacchaeus said, "I'll pay back all I took from people."
   What else did Zacchaeus say?
   Circle his words and print them here.

   ____

2. Jesus told Zacchaeus, "God's forgiveness
   has come to you."
   What else did Jesus say?
   Circle Jesus' words and print them here.

   ____

Circle all the words that you might use to make up with someone you have hurt.

"I'm sorry."

"You're mean."

"I didn't mean to hurt you."

"I'll try never to do that again."

"I don't like you."

"Please forgive me."

"I'll never play with you again!"

"You will always be my friend."

Come, Spirit of God

Sometimes we hurt others.
Sometimes they hurt us.
Jesus gives us the gift of the Holy Spirit.
We can ask the Holy Spirit to help us make up.
We can be at peace with others.

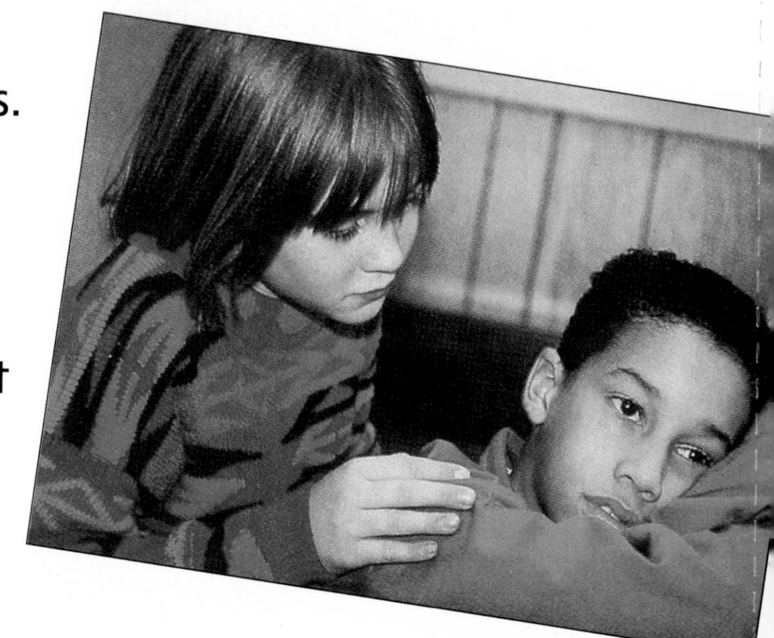

Activity

Look at the pictures.
Tell a story about them.
What do you think
is happening?
What do you think
will happen next?

How can the Holy Spirit
help these people?
How can the people
make up and be at peace?

We Believe

Jesus brings us God's forgiveness and peace. Jesus gives us the Holy Spirit to help us live peacefully together.

Activity

Circle what to say and do to make peace.

Margaret stole Luis' cupcake.
Now Luis is hungry.
What can Margaret do to make peace?

"I'm sorry I lied."

Sam said Lein took his spelling paper.
Then Sam found his paper in his desk.
What can Sam do to make peace?

"Please take my snack."

Amy pushed Johnny on the playground.
Johnny dropped his candy in the sand.
What can Amy do to make peace?

HUG

"Forgive me."

"Let's be friends again."

"Will you play with me?"

"Here's my piece of candy."

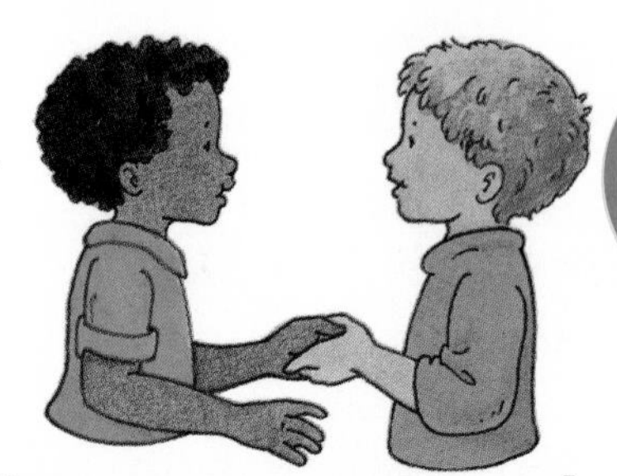

Shake Hands

Invite your friend to your house.

A Sign of Peace

At Mass, Catholics give one
another a sign of peace.
We ask the Holy Spirit to help
make us peacemakers.
We ask the Spirit of God
to help us forgive.
We ask the Holy Spirit
to help us say, "I'm sorry."

Activity

Make a storybook about a child
who hurts someone and is forgiven.
Write the title of your book here.

Praying for Peace

The Holy Spirit helps us make peace.
We can pray to be children of peace.

Dear God,
You made me special.
Help me remember that when
someone hurts me, I am your
special child.
Fill my heart with your peace.

Show me that other people are
special, too.
Help me show them your gentle
peace.
Amen.

Chapter Review

We can make peace with others.

Put the pictures in 1, 2, and 3 order to show forgiveness.

1. Whom did Jesus give us to help live peacefully together?

____

2. What word means to excuse or pardon?

____

3. Talk about what the Holy Spirit can help us do after we hurt someone or after someone hurts us.

Forgive others the way the Lord forgives you.
Based on Colossians 3:13

The Holy Spirit Gives Us Joy

Joy! Joy! Joy!

Make up stories about the children in the pictures. What are they doing to be happy?

What are your favorite fun times?

Activity

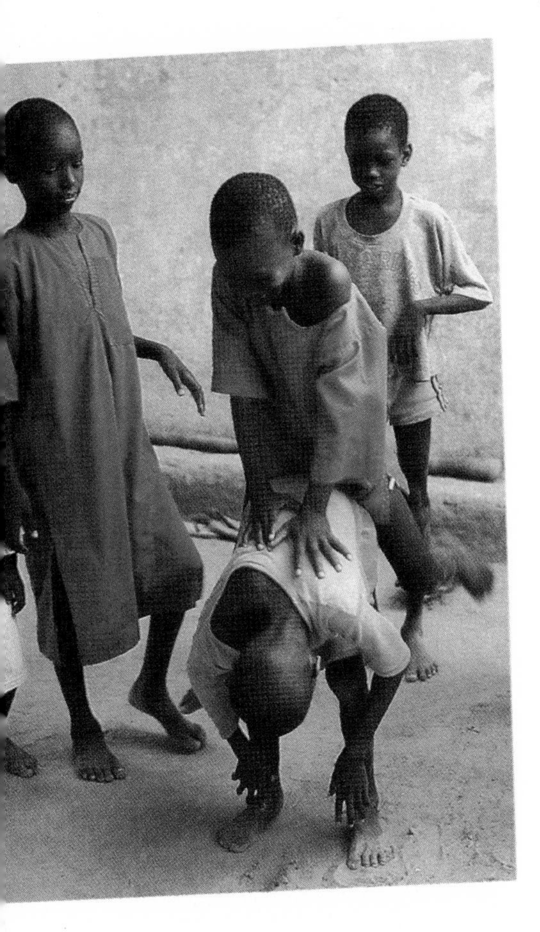

Who helps to make you happy?
What helps to make you happy?
Print the names of the people and things that make you happy here.

Come, Spirit of Joy

God wants us to be happy.
So Jesus gives us the gift of the Holy Spirit.
The Holy Spirit is with us to help us be happy and joyful.

We Believe

**God wants us to be happy.
Jesus gives us the Holy Spirit.
The Holy Spirit comes to give us joy.**

A Dark Night and a Bright Morning

Jesus' friends fished all night
on the Sea of **Galilee**.
They caught nothing.
They were tired and sad.

In the morning a man on the
shore called out to them,
"Try letting your net down on
the right side of the boat."

They did what the man said,
and their net was filled with fish!
Their sadness turned to joy.

"It's Jesus!" John shouted with joy. Peter was so happy that he dived into the lake and swam to Jesus.

Jesus was on the beach cooking breakfast for his friends. They ate bread and fish. They were so glad to see Jesus. They enjoyed the food and were happy being together.

Based on John 21:1–13

Activity

Write one thing that the friends of Jesus did that you would like to do, too.

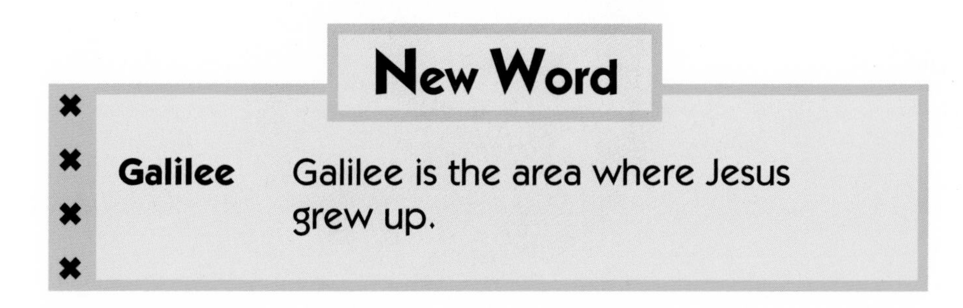

New Word

Galilee Galilee is the area where Jesus grew up.

Happy Times

When the sun is shining
And the birds begin to sing,
I like to take a walk outside
And think of happy things.

I think about my family
And the happy days we've spent,
Like the weekend we went camping
And forgot to bring the tent.

I think about my good friends
And the happy things we do,
Like games and races all for fun
And laughing under skies of blue.

Helping Others Be Happy

The Holy Spirit helps us live as Jesus showed us.
Sometimes the Holy Spirit sends someone to help us.
Sometimes we can be helpers.
The Holy Spirit helps us think of ways to help others.

Activity

Here is a story of a girl who needs help.
Mia is very sad.
She tries and tries to tell time, but it is too hard for her.
Johnny is good at telling time.

In the clock, draw how Johnny can help Mia be happy.

Spreading Joy

Maria has just come to America, and she cannot speak English. On her first day of school, Mrs. Gast taught the children to welcome her. “Bienvenido, Maria,” they said.

Finally, it was time for recess. Mrs. Gast wondered, “How will Maria have fun playing with the children? She cannot understand them.”

Activity

Write what the children can do at recess to help Maria be happy.

Who is always with us, helping us to live like Jesus?

Jesus Spreads Joy

Jesus and some of his friends were out telling people the good news. They were very near to Martha and Mary's house.

Jesus stopped in to visit them. Martha and Mary were happy to see Jesus and his friends.

Everyone sat down and talked. Mary listened to Jesus. She was full of joy.

But Martha was busy cooking for the company. She wanted to be with Jesus, too. "Oh Martha come be with me," said Jesus.

Based on Luke 10:38–42

What do you think happened next? Act out the story and add your ending.

Praying the Glory Be

Christians are full of joy. They believe that God the Father, God the Son, and God the Holy Spirit love them.

Trace the words of a prayer of praise Christians say.

Glory be to the Father

and to the Son

and to the Holy Spirit.

As it was in the beginning,
is now, and ever shall be,
world without end.
Amen.

Chapter Review

The Holy Spirit helps us live like Jesus. In the box below, draw a picture of a time when the Holy Spirit helped you act like Jesus.

1. Whom does Jesus give us to help us be happy?

2. In the gospel story, who was the man on shore?

3. Talk about how you can spread joy and help others feel happy.

Jesus says, "I am with you so you can share my joy."
Based on John 15:11

Unit 5 Organizer

Choose a word to fill in the blank.

The Holy Spirit helps us live as Jesus showed us.

The Holy Spirit helps us . . .

Unit 5 Review

Draw a line to match the words with their meanings.

1. Holy Spirit	the good news of Jesus
2. gospel	excusing or pardoning
3. forgiveness	the Spirit of God

Write an X before the statements that are true.

1. ______ Jesus does not want us to be sorry for hurting others.
2. ______ Jesus gives us the Holy Spirit to make us sad.
3. ______ Jesus always forgives us.
4. ______ The Holy Spirit helps us to live like Jesus.
5. ______ The Holy Spirit comes to give us God's joy.

Circle the names of three gifts that the Holy Spirit gives to us.

joy	sadness	strength
fear	peace	anger

Unit 5 Review

Write the name of the gift Jesus brought to the people in each Bible story.

Peace joy strength

1. The friends of Jesus were afraid of the storm.

2. Jesus shared breakfast with his friends.

3. Jesus brought forgiveness to Zacchaeus.

Talk about the questions below.

1. Why is it important to say we are sorry when we hurt other people?
2. Why is it important to forgive people who hurt us?
3. How does the Holy Spirit help us to be happy?

COPING WITH FEELING SAD

Can you tell how the students in this picture are feeling?

Some students in this picture are feeling

______________________________.

Some students in this picture are feeling

______________________________.

Activity

Draw a picture of something you can do when you feel sad.

Following Jesus

Jesus is always with me.
When I'm sad, I can pray to Jesus to help me feel happier.

Write a prayer to tell Jesus your feelings.

Growing Closer

ENCOURAGE your child to volunteer to help you around the house. This is one way a young child can begin to contribute to the joy of others.

SET ASIDE A TIME for you and your child to talk about some happy and unhappy times you each have had. Discuss what made these times joyous or unpleasant. Plan ways to work on happy times together.

Looking Ahead

Summer is about to begin. From time to time, observe your child at play, helping him or her to understand that taking turns and sharing toys and games are ways to show love as Jesus asked us to do. Continue the religious practices that your child learned in the first grade. Incorporate the prayers in the back of your child's religion book into your family prayertime. Have an enjoyable summer!

OPENING DOORS

A Take-Home Magazine™

THE MASS IS ENDED

Ascension Thursday
(fortieth day after Easter)
This holy day commemorates the ascension of Jesus into heaven which completes his passion, death, and resurrection.

Assumption of Mary
August 15
Since the seventh century, Catholics celebrated the taking of Mary, body and soul, into heaven at the end of her life.

All Saints' Day
November 1
This feast remembers all the saints in heaven, especially those who are not honored on any other day of the year.

The Immaculate Conception
December 8
This day honors Mary who was conceived without original sin.

As you can see, holy days have been added to the Church calendar over the centuries or their dates have been changed. In recent years, the bishops proposed reducing the number of holy days to three. They suggested retaining either Christmas, the Solemnity of Mary, and the Ascension or Christmas, All Saints' Day, and the Immaculate Conception. If you were polled, for which holy days would you vote?

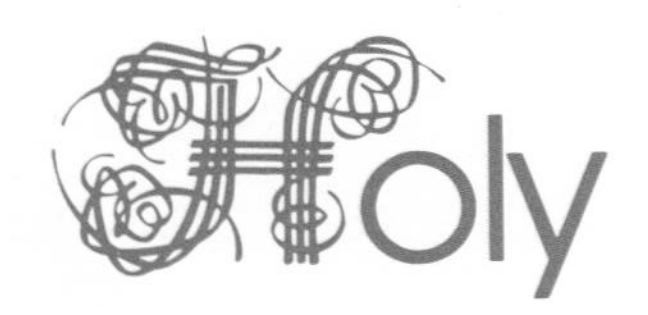oly ays

In former centuries, Church holy days were real *holidays.* People abstained from all work and attended Mass just as they did on Sunday. After Mass, there was often a daylong festival with rich foods, singing, and dancing. Today, holy days are often forgotten as we battle morning traffic, work the late shift, keep appointments, or chauffeur children to after-school activities.

Most of us are familiar with the names and dates of the six holy days of obligation. Did you know, however, that there are really ten holy days observed throughout the universal Church? Each country's bishops have decided upon which of the ten days the local Church will celebrate. The other four holy days observed in some countries other than the United States are: Epiphany, Corpus Christi, the Feast of Saint Joseph, and the Feast of Saints Peter and Paul. In the United States, Catholics celebrate the following six holy days of obligation.

Christmas
December 25
Originally celebrated on January 6, the Feast of the Epiphany, this feast was changed to December 25 to offset pagan sun ceremonies that celebrated the winter solstice.

Solemnity of Mary, Mother of God
January 1
This ancient feast, restored in 1969, honors the Mother of God during the Christmas season.

"Then, after singing a hymn, they went out."

Mark 14:26

These are the concluding words of Mark's account of the Last Supper. The disciples had just experienced one of the greatest moments in their relationship with Jesus—the promise that their Master would be present to them each time they gathered at the table. The gospel account doesn't allow us even a glimpse into the disciples' emotions, but we can probably safely assume that the disciples were deeply touched by the supper events and felt closer to Jesus because of it. However, in the hours that followed, some of them doubted Jesus; one betrayed him, one denied him, a few believed and followed him to Calvary. The disciples had met their greatest challenge—to stay faithful to the Master—and many of them failed the test.

Each Sunday, we, too, leave the Mass, the sacred meal by which we celebrate the Lord's Supper. The celebrant commissions us,

"Go in peace to love and serve the Lord."

This is far more than "farewell until we meet again." The word *Mass* means "to send." We believe that when the Mass is ended, it has really just begun. We are sent to carry the message of the gospel into our homes, the workplace, onto the golf courses, and into the beauty salon. This is not always easy, and our good intentions, like those of the disciples, may meet very challenging circumstances.

As we start out for home, we can claim Jesus' promised Spirit as our companion for the journey. God's power strengthens us, guides us, and gladdens each step we take to share faith and life generously with others. When we consider that the Holy Spirit is with us to help us live out the gospel, we can respond to the words of the Dismissal, "Thanks be to God."

A Closer Look

The Holy Spirit Helps Me

The Dismissal Rite—the ending of the Mass—is the part that challenges us the most. Our celebration is over. How will we live out the celebration until we gather again?

Read these pages with your child. How will you and your family live out the eucharistic celebration during the rest of the week?

Read-Along
At Mass I celebrate Jesus' great love for me.
I thank Jesus for all that he has done for me.
I praise him for the gift of Eucharist.

The Mass is ended.
The priest says,
"Go in peace to love and serve the Lord."

The Holy Spirit will help me love others.
The Holy Spirit will give me strength,
peace, and joy.

I pray,

Thanks be to God.

This is a picture of how my family will celebrate Jesus this week.

The next time you go to Mass, remember to pray aloud the prayer you have just learned.

Celebrating the Journey

Leader Dear God, we like being on a journey with you.
It is exciting and full of your love.
We thank you for being with us.

Children God is with us always.

Leader Our journey is not over.
It will go on all summer and all through our lives.
God the Father will be with us.
God the Son will be with us.
God the Holy Spirit will always help us.

Children God is with us always.

All Amen.

A
M

Our Church Celebrates Advent

A Time of Waiting

God made a promise long ago.
God promised to send Jesus.
The people waited many years
for Jesus, God's Son.
Then God sent Jesus to show us
how to live as children of God.

During **Advent** we wait, too.
We wait for Jesus.
We prepare our minds and
hearts for Christmas.

We pray,
"O Lord Jesus, come! Be with us."

Based on I Corinthians 16:22

Activity

1. Color the Advent wreath.
2. Read the words on the candles.
3. Then write the words on the line below.

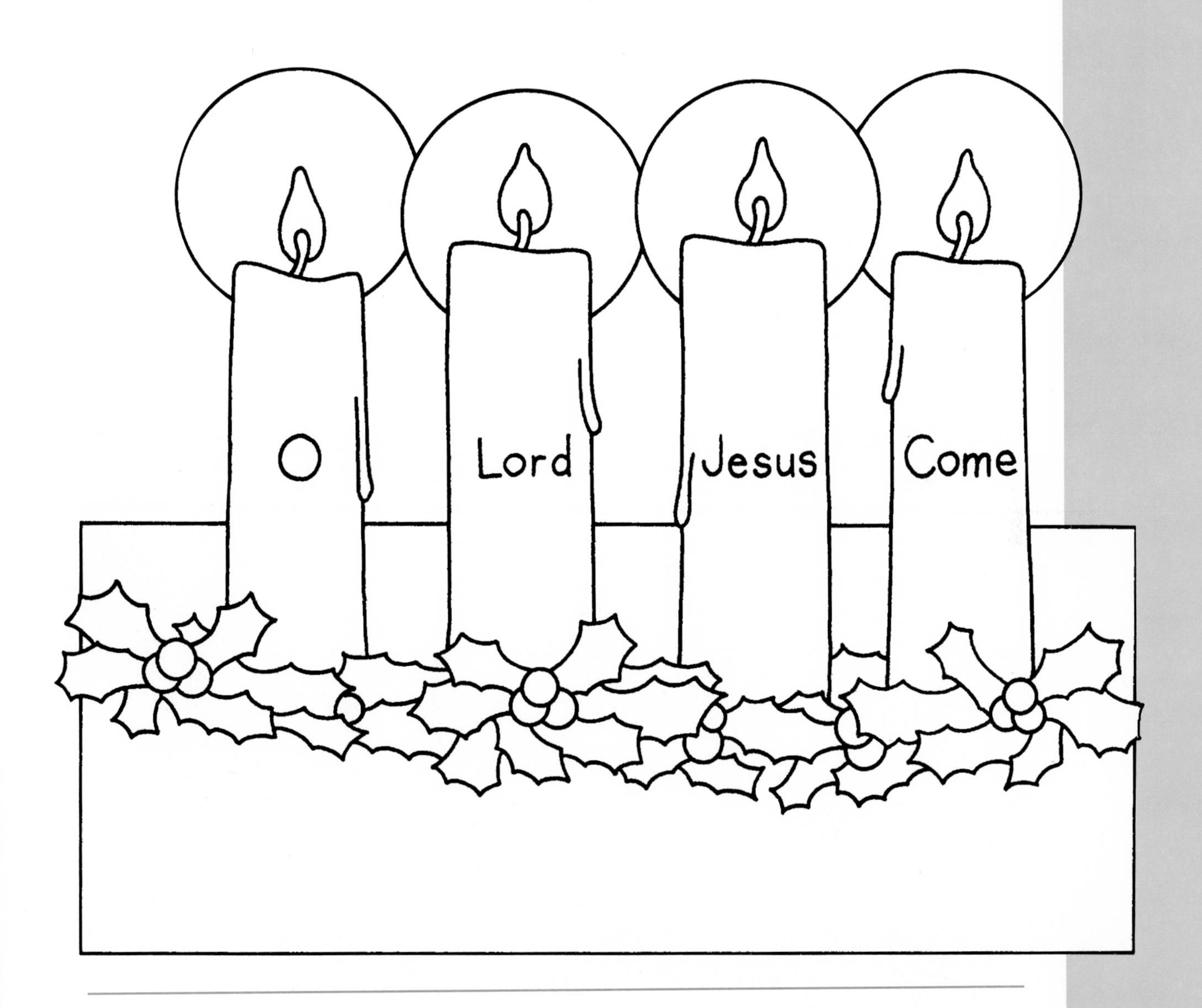

We Welcome Jesus

Four, three, two, one—
Count the weeks till Jesus comes.
Each week we add another light,
Our hope for Jesus glowing bright.
We pray, we share, we do our part,
To welcome Jesus in our hearts.

The Advent wreath helps us prepare
for Jesus' birthday.
We light a candle and pray together.
Soon all four candles are lighted.

Draw a picture of yourself during Advent. Show how you will welcome Jesus.

Trace the letters below that show you want God to be with us.

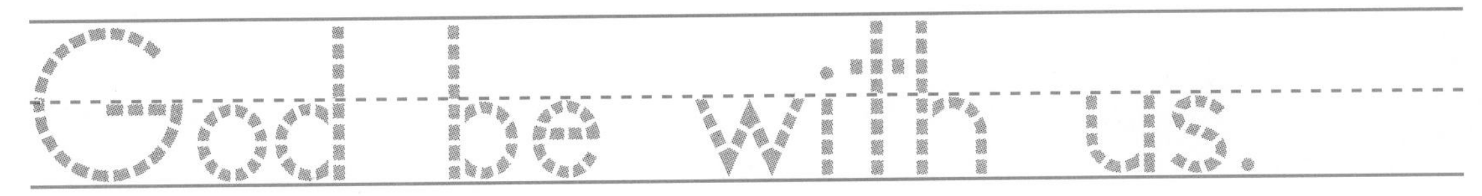

God Be with Us!

Jesus is called **Emmanuel**.
Emmanuel means "God is with us."
We call Jesus "Emmanuel" because
Jesus is God who came to be with us.

During Advent we get ready
for Christmas.
We prepare for the coming
of Jesus.

We prepare for Emmanuel
by trying to be more loving.
We get ready by helping others.

As we prepare for the coming
of Emmanuel, we are full of joy.
We wait for Jesus, God's great
gift to us.

Activity

Put an **X** by the pictures that show how you get ready for Jesus.

We light another candle for each week of waiting.

We prepare a food basket for God's poor.

We get our house ready to celebrate Jesus with us.

We set up a crib to remember what we are waiting for.

An Advent Chain

Make an Advent chain.
It will help you prepare for Jesus' birthday.
Each time you do something to show your love, add another link.

1. Your teacher will give you strips of paper, crayons, and glue.

2. On each strip of paper, draw a picture that shows how you care.

3. Glue the ends of one strip together to form a circle. Add the other links to the chain.

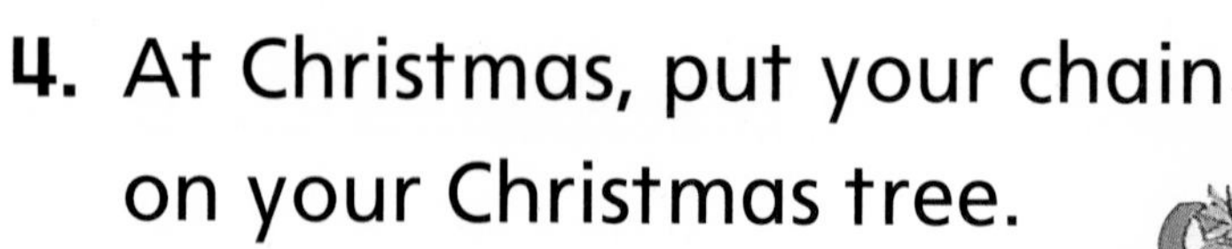

4. At Christmas, put your chain on your Christmas tree.

An Advent Prayer Service

Teacher	We will name the Advent candles. We will call the first candle promise. When we light the first candle, we pray,
Children	O Jesus, you are God's promise to us.
Teacher	We call the second candle hope. When we light the second candle, we pray,
Children	O Jesus, we wait in hope for you.
Teacher	The third candle we call joy. When we light the third candle, we pray,
Children	O Jesus, you bring joy to the world.
Teacher	The fourth candle we call love. When we light the fourth candle, we pray,
Children	O Jesus, you teach us how to love.

Our Church Celebrates Christmas

A Time for Giving

Christmas is the birthday of Jesus.
We give gifts to our family and friends.
They give gifts to us, too.

These gifts remind us of Jesus.
He is our greatest gift from God.
Jesus gives us gifts of love and peace.
We share these gifts with others on Christmas.

We pray, "Glory to God! Peace to all people."

Based on Luke 2:14

Activity

Look at the picture.
Write the correct word on the line below
to finish the sentence.

God the Father's greatest gift to us is

______________________________, our Savior.

The First Christmas

Mary and Joseph went to Bethlehem.
The town was crowded with people.
Mary and Joseph had no place to sleep.
They found a barn, and Joseph made a straw bed for Mary.

That night, Jesus was born.
Mary wrapped Jesus in warm clothes.
Joseph found a wooden box and filled it with clean hay.
Joseph used the box as a crib for baby Jesus.
Mary and Joseph watched Jesus sleep.
They rejoiced and thanked God for Jesus.

Based on Luke 2:1–7

Activity

Find the hidden words. Color them green.
Then color the picture.

A Family Christmas Celebration

After Christmas Mass, Dean
and his dad went to pick up
Grandma at the nursing home.

Dean kissed her and said, "We
have a fruit basket for the nurses.
We have surprises for your friends!"
Dad wheeled Grandma around as
Dean happily passed out the presents.

When they got home, the family
ate a big Christmas dinner.
After dinner they gathered
around the tree for dessert.
It was a beautiful Christmas cake.

Then the family gave Grandma her presents and sang Christmas carols. Dean said, “I love Jesus’ birthday.”

Activity

Here is Dean’s family Christmas cake. Print the missing word on the cake. Then decorate the cake.

A Christmas Ornament

1. Your teacher will give you a balloon and some wet yarn.
2. Blow up the balloon and tie it tight.
3. Wrap yarn around the balloon so that the balloon is covered with yarn.
4. When the yarn dries, pop the balloon. Now you have a Christmas ornament.

At Christmas we give gifts to spread Jesus' love. To whom will you give your Christmas ornament?

A Christmas Prayer Service

Dear Jesus,
I will give you a gift.
It is a gift from my heart.
It is a gift of love.

My gift is ______________________.

We pray,
Thank you, God, for Jesus.
Help us to remember
all your gifts.
Help us to give the gift of
ourselves to others.
Glory to God!
Amen.

Our Church Celebrates Lent

The First Day of Lent

We get ready for Easter during Lent.
Ash Wednesday is the first day of Lent.

On **Ash Wednesday,** the priest traces the sign of the cross on our foreheads with ashes.
The ashes remind us to follow Jesus.
We should try to be more like Jesus.

We pray, "I will follow Jesus."

Activity

Find the hidden picture.
Color each shape with a *.

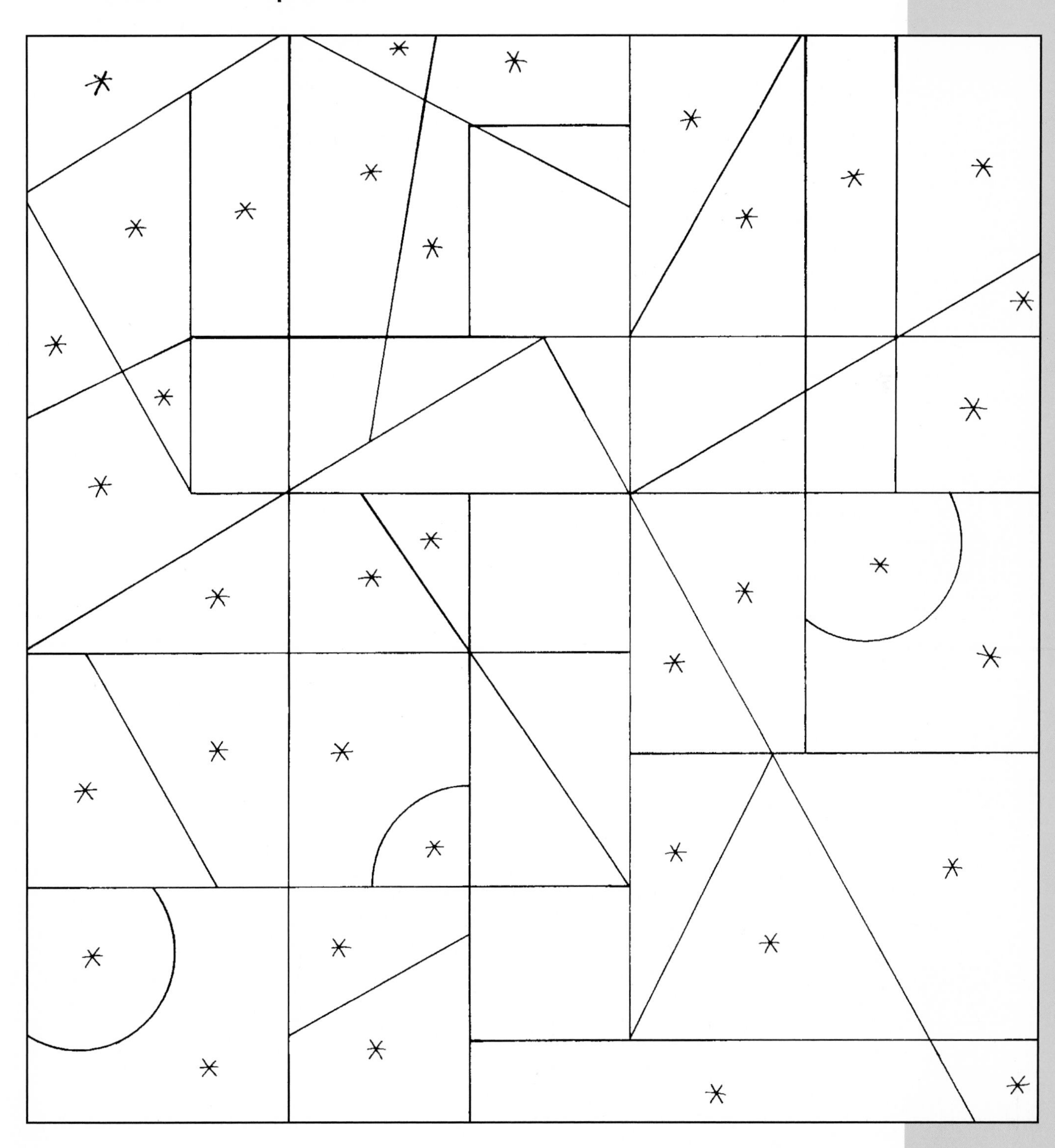

A Time to Become More Like Jesus

Tim and Amy were fighting.
Tim wanted to watch one
TV show.
Amy wanted to watch a
different show.
Then Tim remembered
that it was **Lent**.
He remembered that he was trying to be
loving and forgiving.
Tim was trying to become more like Jesus.

How could Tim be like Jesus?
Draw a picture showing what Tim could do.

Activity

Put an **X** next to the pictures that show children trying to be like Jesus.
Then trace the words below.

Jesus says,

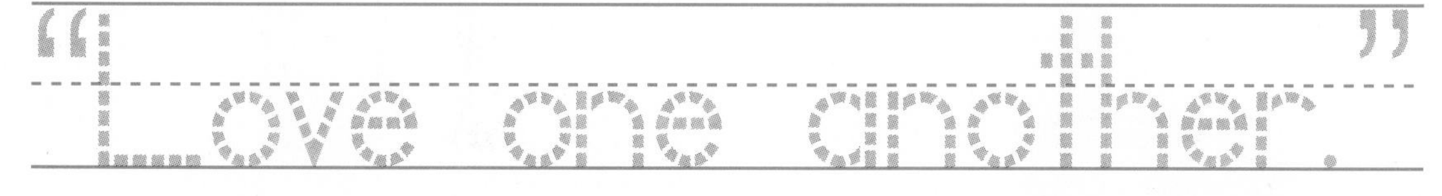

Based on John 13:34

We Follow Jesus

Jesus, we will follow you,
Follow you, follow you.
Jesus we will follow you,
All the way to Easter.

Lent is a time to help and share,
A time to pray, a time to love.
We will show our love for you,
All the way to Easter.

Lent lasts all of forty days,
Forty days, forty days.
How will we act for forty days
To show our love for Jesus?

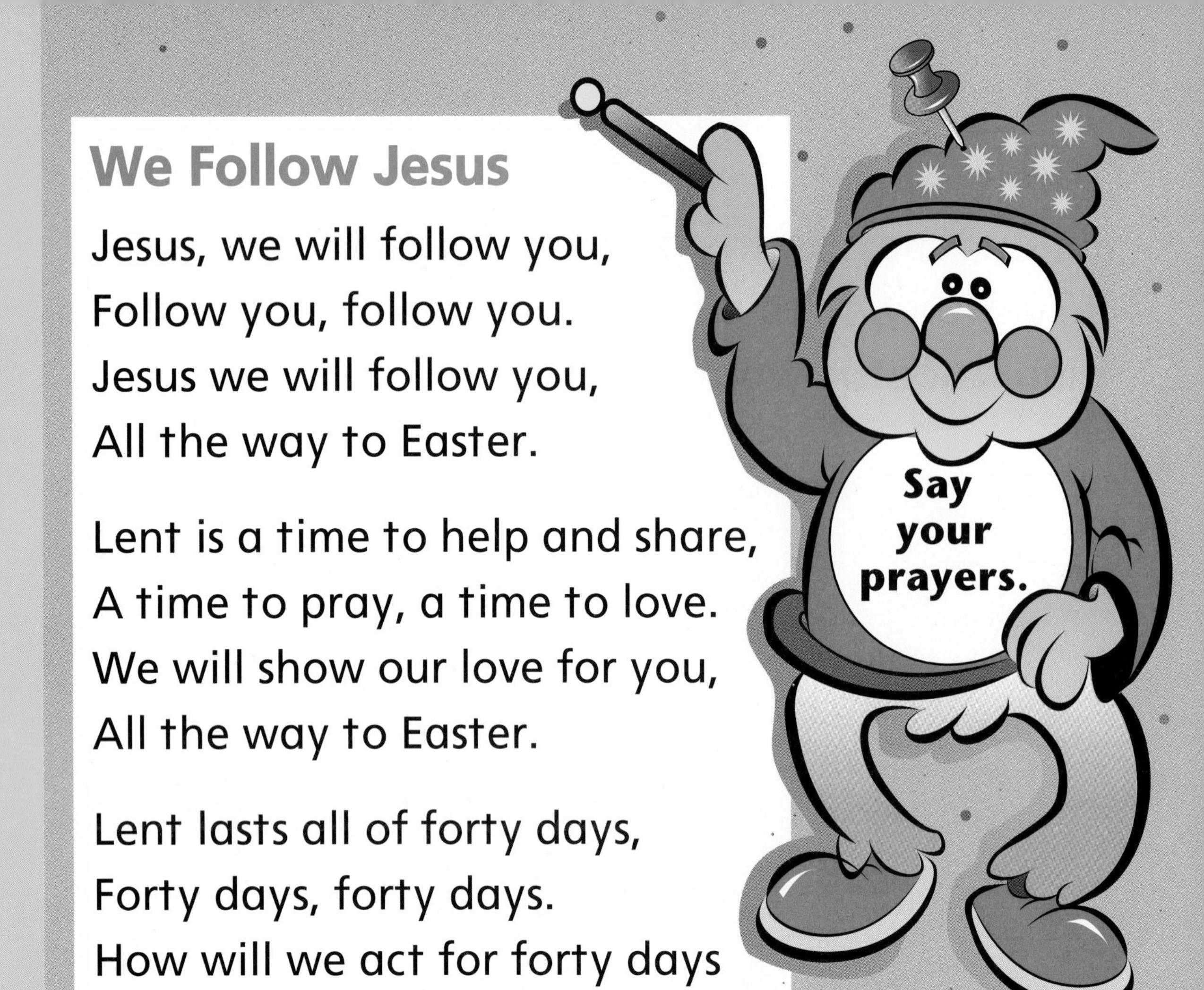

Activity
How will you show love during the forty days of Lent?
Finish coloring the memo pad each time you try to be more like Jesus.
Help a friend.
Obey your parents.
Make a get-well card.
Share your toys.

Our Journey with Jesus

During Lent we are on a journey
with Jesus.
On our journey to Easter, we think
about how we are living.

Sometimes we do not show
our love for Jesus.
Sometimes we are selfish.
Sometimes we hurt others.
During Lent we think about how to act.

We try to change the things that keep
us from being as loving as Jesus.
Jesus will help us say we are sorry to
the people we have hurt.
He will help us make up and be friends again.

Looking at How We Live

Let's think about how we act.
Do you need to say, "I'm sorry," and
make up with someone?
Can you say, "I try to love as Jesus asks us"?

I say my prayers every day.

I tell the truth.

I fight with my friends.

I help at home.

I take things that don't belong to me.

I share my toys.

I take care of my things.

I am mean to others.

I say, "I'm sorry," when I hurt others.

I obey my parents and teachers.

A Special Sign of Lent

The cross reminds us of Jesus.
It helps us remember to be
loving and forgiving.
Make a cross to remind you
to be more like Jesus.

1. Your teacher will give you a paper cross and pieces of colored paper.

2. Tear the pieces of paper into smaller pieces.

3. Paste the pieces all over the paper cross.

4. Share the cross with your family.

A Prayer Service for Lent

Teacher Jesus, you were kind to others.

Children I will follow you, Jesus.

Teacher Jesus, you show us how to love.

Children I will follow you, Jesus.

Teacher Jesus, you thought of others first.

Children I will follow you, Jesus.

All Help us to follow you, Jesus.
Help us to love one another.
Amen.

Our Church Celebrates Holy Week

Passion Sunday

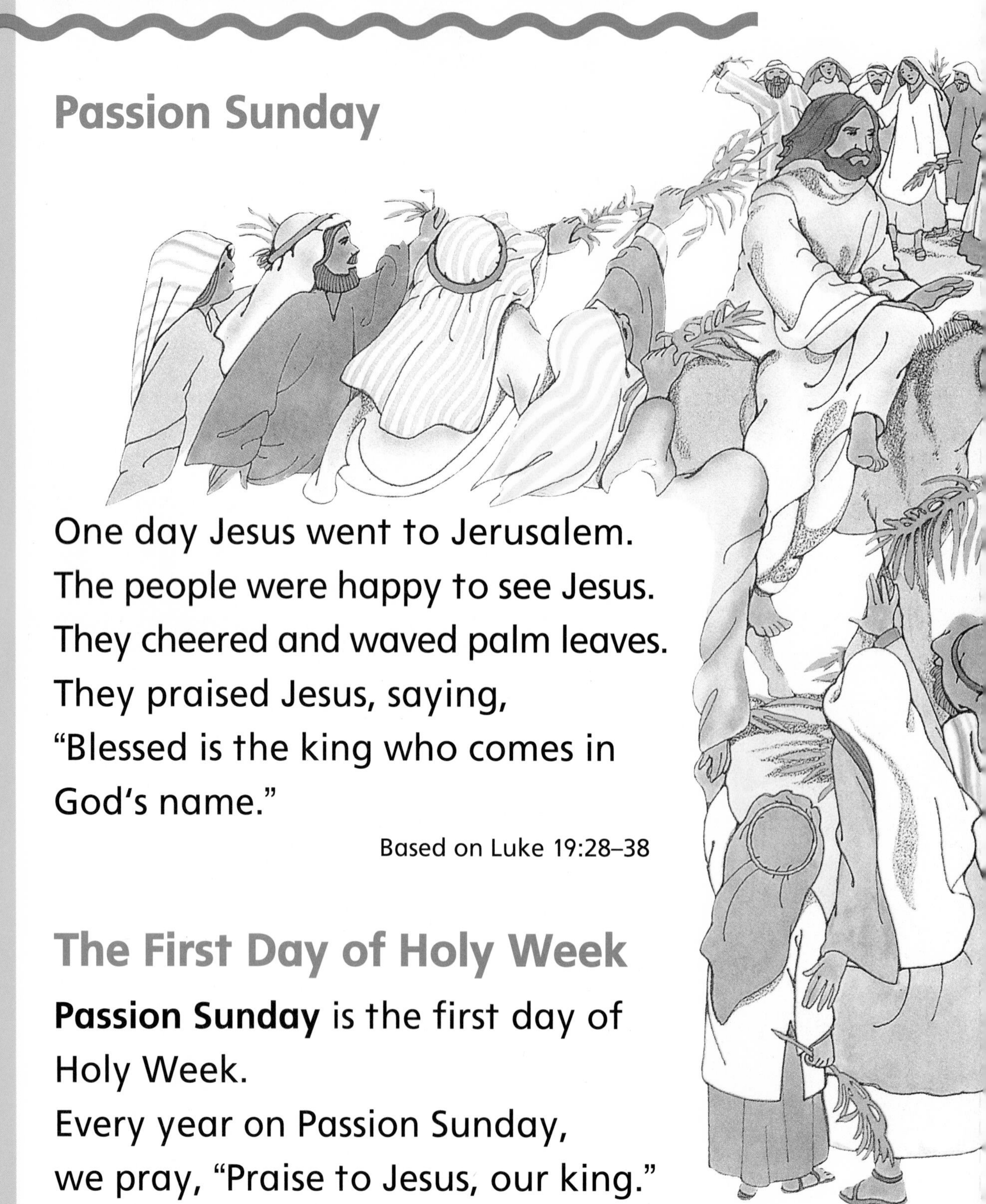

One day Jesus went to Jerusalem.
The people were happy to see Jesus.
They cheered and waved palm leaves.
They praised Jesus, saying,
"Blessed is the king who comes in God's name."

Based on Luke 19:28–38

The First Day of Holy Week

Passion Sunday is the first day of Holy Week.
Every year on Passion Sunday, we pray, "Praise to Jesus, our king."

Finish this prayer by drawing a picture in each box.

Jesus, we praise you

in the morning.	at night.

Jesus, you are our king. 

The Holiest Days of the Year

When Lent is over, we celebrate the
three most important days of the year.

On **Holy Thursday** we celebrate the
special meal when Jesus said,
"This is my body. This is my blood."

Then Jesus told his friends that he was
going to die soon.
But he promised that he would
rise from the dead.

After the holy meal, Jesus and his
friends went to a garden to pray.
There soldiers came to arrest him.

On **Good Friday** we remember
the day Jesus died on the cross.

After Jesus died and was buried, a
wonderful thing happened to him.
God the Father raised Jesus to new life.

On **Holy Saturday** night we begin
our Easter celebration.
We celebrate Jesus' rising to new life.
We keep celebrating on **Easter Sunday**.

Activity

During these three holy days, we think of Jesus and the cross.
Starting with the letter "I", copy the colored letters on the line below.
Write what Jesus tells us during these holy days.

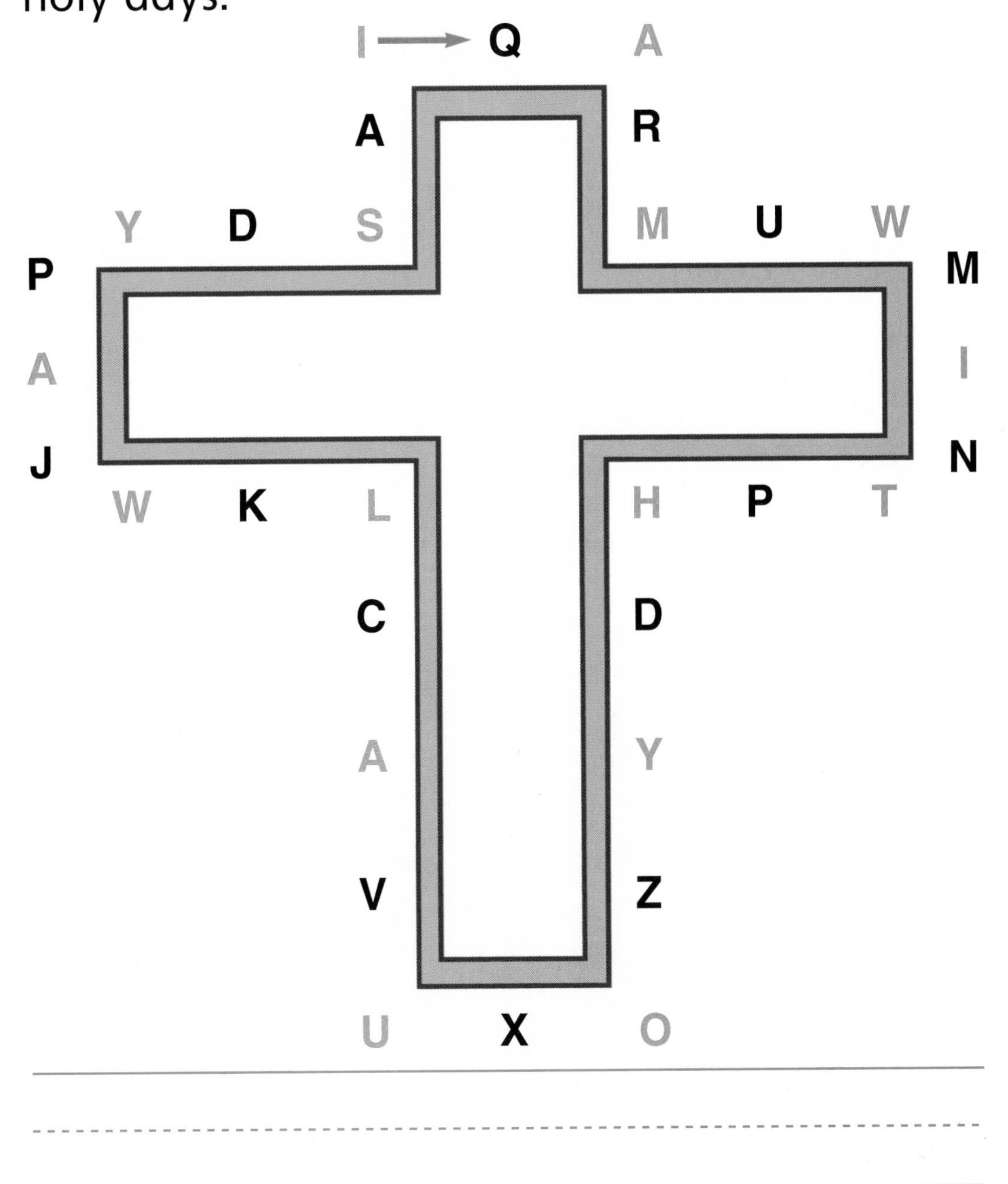

Our Church Celebrates Easter

A Time for Joy

Jesus died.
His friends were very sad.
They buried him in a special place.
Three days later, Jesus' friends visited this special place.

But Jesus' body was not there.
Jesus is alive again.
He is risen.
We continue our celebration of Jesus' new life on Easter Sunday.

On Easter we pray, "Alleluia! Jesus is alive."

Activity

Talk about the pictures and the words.
Write the words on the lines below.

Jesus gives us new life and joy.

A Sign of New Life

It was Easter Sunday.
Tina and her family went to Mass.
Father Jim lit the Easter candle.
He said, "This is a sign of new life.
Jesus shares his new life with us."

Later everyone sang together.
They sang, "Alleluia! Alleluia!
Jesus is alive!
Praise to the Lord!"

On Easter we pray,
"Thank you, Jesus for being with us.
Alleluia!"

Activity

Connect the dots and color the picture.
Then trace the word below.

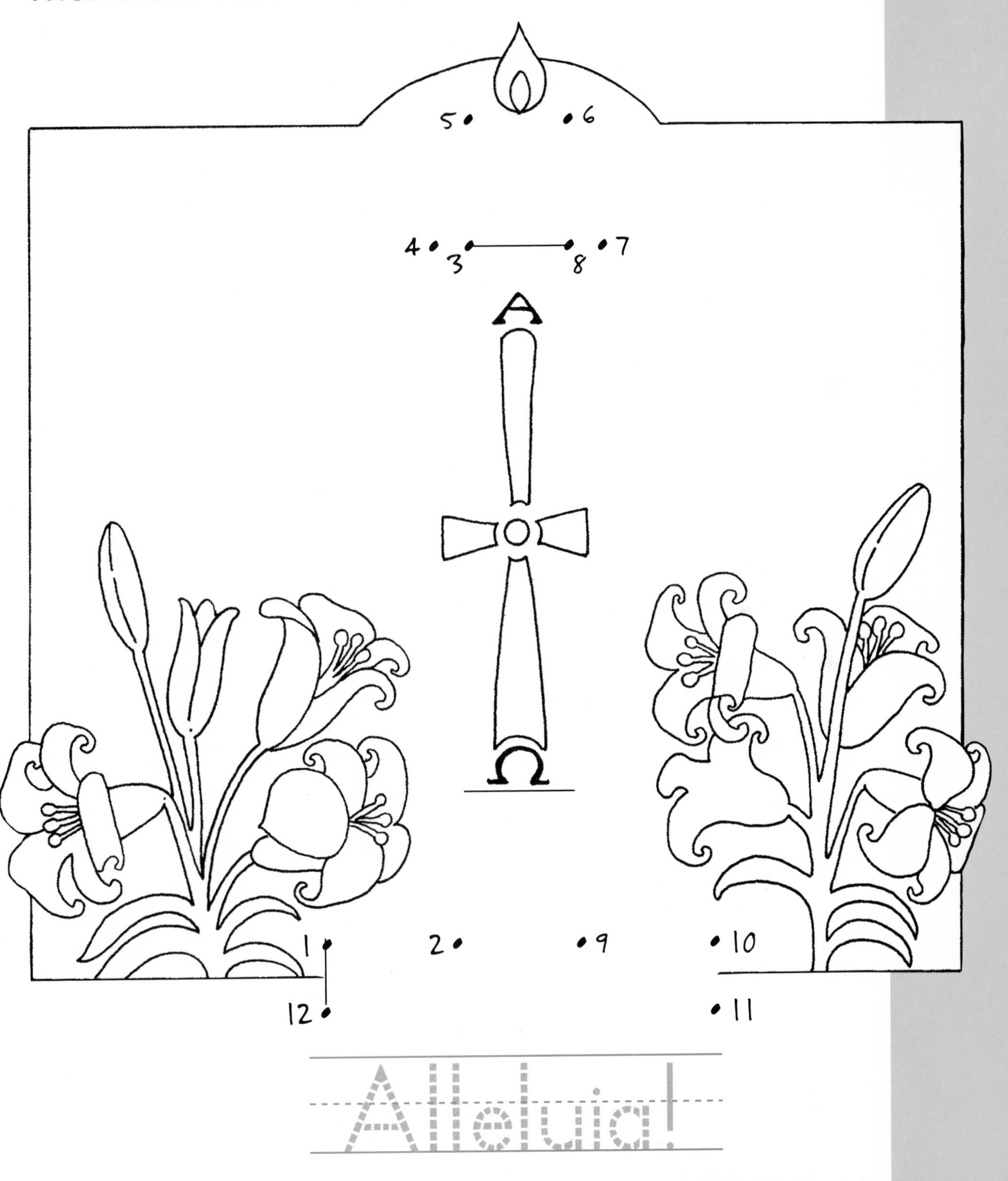

Alleluia!

An Easter Play

Narrator Mary Magdala went to Jesus' tomb, the place he was buried. Jesus was not there, so Mary cried. An angel who was sitting there saw her crying.

Angel "Why are you crying?"

Mary "Someone has taken Jesus away."

Narrator Mary turned and saw a man. She thought he was the gardener. Mary did not know it, but the man was Jesus.

Jesus "Why are you crying? Whom are you looking for?"

Mary "Tell me where Jesus is. I will go there."

Jesus "Mary!"

Narrator Mary looked at the man again.
Now she knew he was Jesus.
Full of joy, Mary ran to him.

Mary "Teacher!"

Narrator Mary saw that Jesus had risen
from the dead.
She rushed to tell Jesus' other
friends.

Mary "I have seen Jesus.
He is alive!"

Based on John 20:11–18

An Easter Book

Make an Easter book for someone you love.
Tell them, “Jesus is alive! Happy Easter!”

1. Your teacher will give you paper and crayons.
2. Draw a picture of Jesus and his friends.
   Draw pictures of new life.
   Draw a picture of yourself that shows how you feel about Easter.
3. Write a prayer to Jesus thanking him for sharing his new life with you.
4. Your teacher will help you put the pages of your Easter book together.

An Easter Prayer Service

All Jesus said, "Remember,
I am with you always."

Based on Matthew 28:20

Teacher We love you, Jesus.

Children Your new life shines in us.

Teacher On Easter we remember
your love for us.

Children We will try to share
your love.

Teacher Jesus, be with us today
and every day.

Children Amen.

Our Church Honors Saints

Saint Joseph

God gave **Joseph** a very special job to do.
Joseph did what God asked him.
He was the husband of Mary and helped her take care of Jesus.

Joseph worked as a carpenter.
His shop was in the Holy Family's home in Nazareth.
He taught Jesus how to make things with wood.

Joseph was a very good man.
He loved Jesus and Mary.
And they loved Joseph very much.

We honor Saint Joseph on March 19 and May 1.
On these days, we pray,
"Saint Joseph, help us lead good lives."

Activity

Jesus liked to help Joseph.
Connect the dots to find something
Joseph and Jesus made together.
Start at number **1**.
Then color the picture.

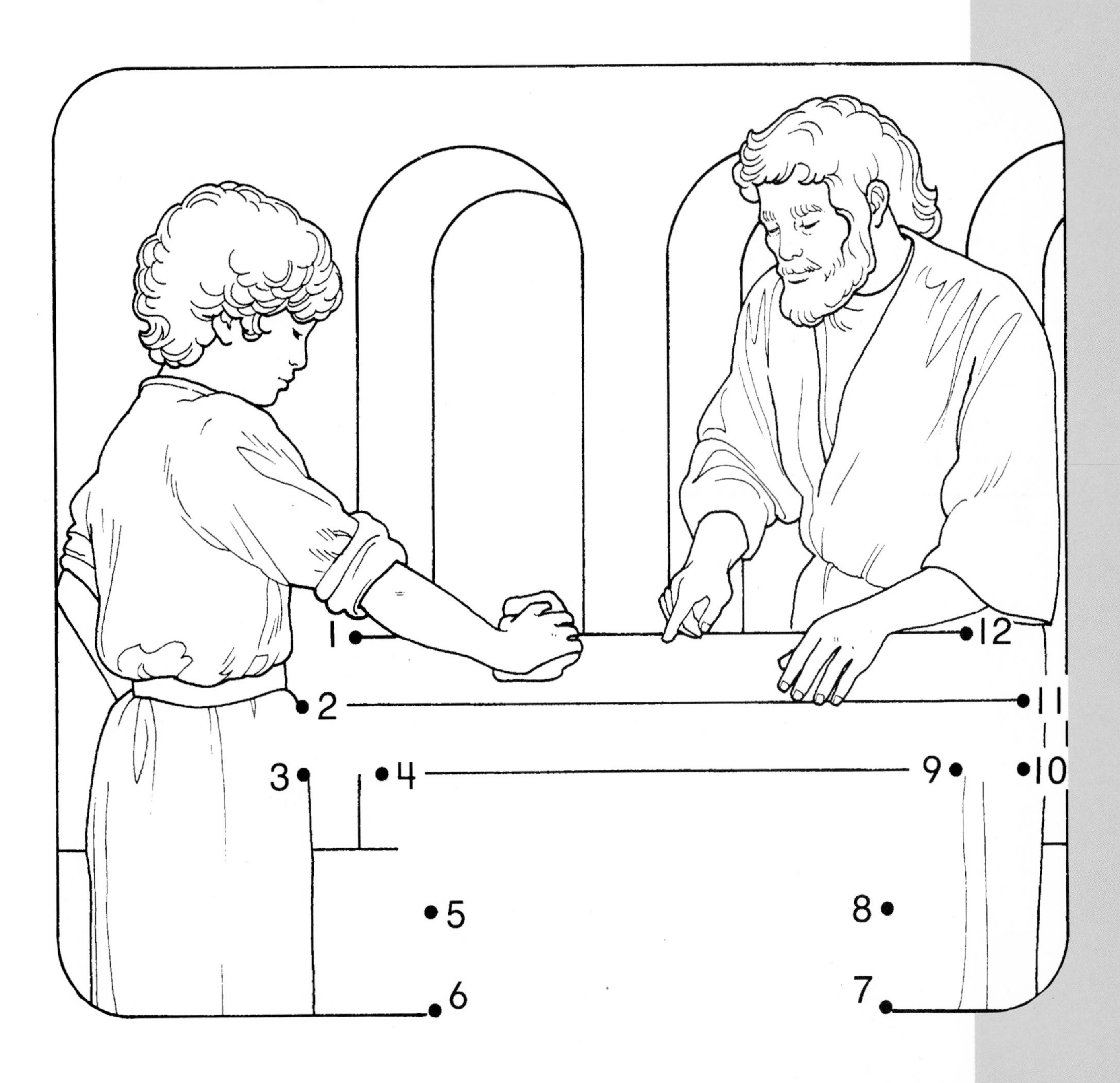

Saint Nicholas

Little Nicholas shared his toys and food.
When he grew up, he gave all his money away.

Nicholas became a bishop.
He loved God, and he loved children very much.
He helped them and was kind to them.
To help them he sometimes gave them gifts.
People told stories about Saint Nicholas
and his good deeds.

Like Nicholas, they gave gifts to each other.
They shared and helped each other.

We honor Saint Nicholas on December 6.
We pray, "Saint Nicholas, help us to do kind
things for others."

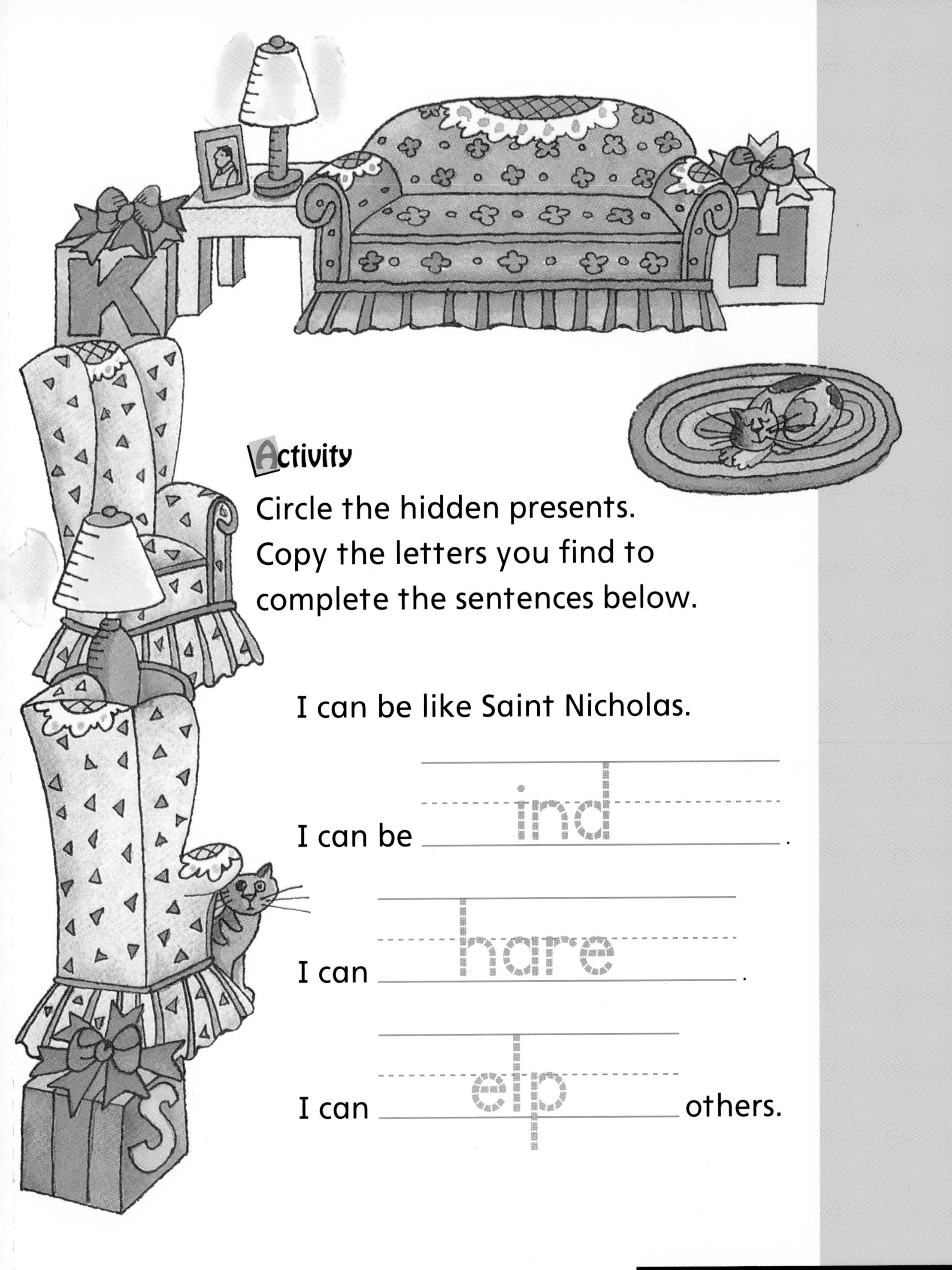

Activity

Circle the hidden presents.
Copy the letters you find to
complete the sentences below.

I can be like Saint Nicholas.

I can be ind.

I can hare.

I can elp others.

Saint Rose of Lima

Isabel was a beautiful baby.
People said that she was as
beautiful as a rose.
So everyone called her "Rose."

Rose came from a poor family
in South America.
She grew flowers from tiny seeds.
She sold the flowers to earn
money to help her family.

Rose showed her love for God
by helping others.
She made one room in her house
into a hospital.
She brought sick children and
old people to her hospital.
Rose helped them get better.

We honor Saint Rose of Lima
on August 23.
She was the first saint of both
North and South America.

Activity

Rose liked to sew.
She used a needle and thread
to make pictures and words on cloth.
Color the threads on the cloth below
and find Saint Rose's favorite prayer.

A Diorama

It is fun to make stand-up scenes of a story inside a box.
Make a scene of a story of your favorite saint.

1. Get a box with a lid that comes off.
   A shoe box is good.

2. Think of a story of your favorite saint.
   Where is the saint?
   Who else is there?

3. Make stand-up characters from tagboard.

4. Stand the characters up in the scene.
   Add furniture for an inside scene.
   Add flowers and trees if it is outside.

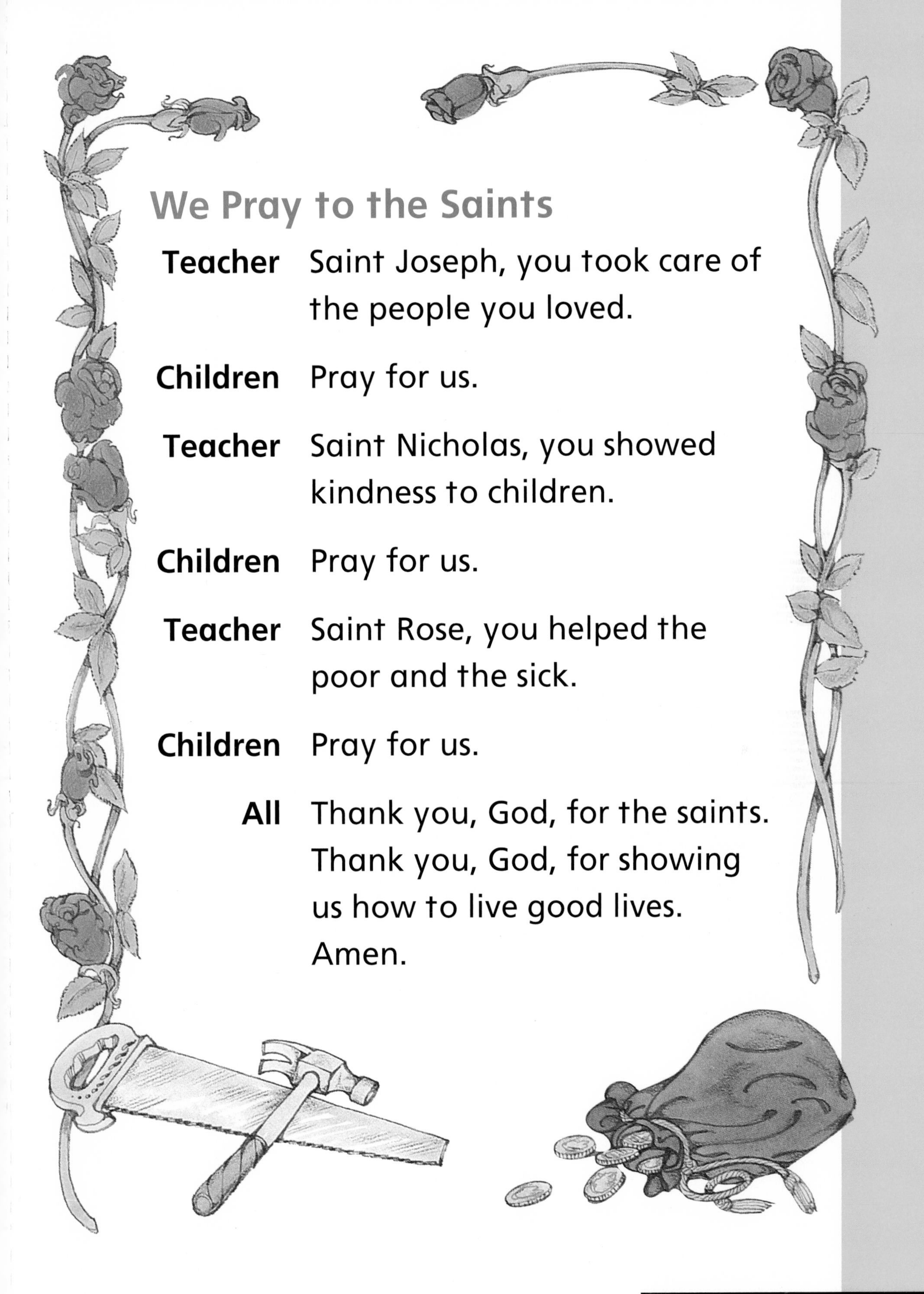

We Pray to the Saints

Teacher Saint Joseph, you took care of the people you loved.

Children Pray for us.

Teacher Saint Nicholas, you showed kindness to children.

Children Pray for us.

Teacher Saint Rose, you helped the poor and the sick.

Children Pray for us.

All Thank you, God, for the saints. Thank you, God, for showing us how to live good lives. Amen.

Our Church Honors Mary

The Month of Mary

Mary was the mother of Jesus.
She cared for Jesus.
Jesus loved Mary.
Jesus wants us to love Mary, too.

We remember Mary during
the month of May.
We try to be like her.

We pray,
"Hail Mary, full of grace,
The Lord is with you.
Blessed are you among women
and blessed is the fruit
of your womb, Jesus."

Based on Luke 1:28, 42

Activity

Color the picture of Mary. Trace the letters of the words below.

Holy Mary,
Mother of God

The Birth of Mary

Anne and Joachim were kind and good.
They asked God to bless them with a baby.
They prayed and prayed.
They waited for a long time.
Finally Anne gave birth to a baby girl.

Anne and Joachim named their new baby girl Mary.
Mary was part of God's promise to us.
She grew up to be the mother of Jesus.

We honor Mary's birth on September 8.
We pray, "Help us grow in our love for Jesus."

Activity

Color all the spaces with an **X** blue.
What does the puzzle say?

The May Crowning

It was May crowning, a special
ceremony to honor Mary.
The children walked into church in
a long line called a **procession**.
They sang hymns to Mary.
They listened to stories about Mary
from the Bible.

Then the children gathered around
a beautiful statue of Mary.
One of the eighth graders put a
wreath of flowers on Mary's head.

The first-grade children prayed,
"Loving Mary, Mother dear,
Keep your children always near.
Help us as we work and play.
Be with us now and every day."

Activity

You have learned many things about Mary this year.
Draw a line to match the words below with the pictures.

Mary's mother and father — Gabriel

Mary's son — Joseph

God's messenger who came to Mary — Joachim and Anne

Mary's husband — Jesus

Our Church Celebrates Holy Days

The Epiphany

After Jesus was born, some wise men saw a new star in the sky. They thought the star was a sign that a new king was born. They wanted to see the new king.

The wise men followed the star. Finally, the star stopped over the stable where Jesus was born. The wise men went into the stable to see Jesus. They knew he was a special person sent by God. They praised him and gave him gifts.

Based on Matthew 2:1–11

Our Guiding Light

On the feast of the **Epiphany**, we pray, "Jesus, may the light of your love always lead us."

Activity

Help the children to find their way to Jesus.
Use a yellow crayon.

The Feast Of Saint Francis

Francis' family was very rich.
His family gave him everything he wanted.
Francis was a soldier and was captured.
He was put in jail.
There he thought a lot about God.
He learned that God was more
important than money.

So Francis gave away his beautiful
clothes and dressed like a poor man.
He gave his money to those who needed it.

In his new life, Saint Francis spent a
lot of time talking to Jesus in prayer.

He made many new friends and they
went from town to town, helping people.
Francis loved everyone and called all
people his brothers and sisters.

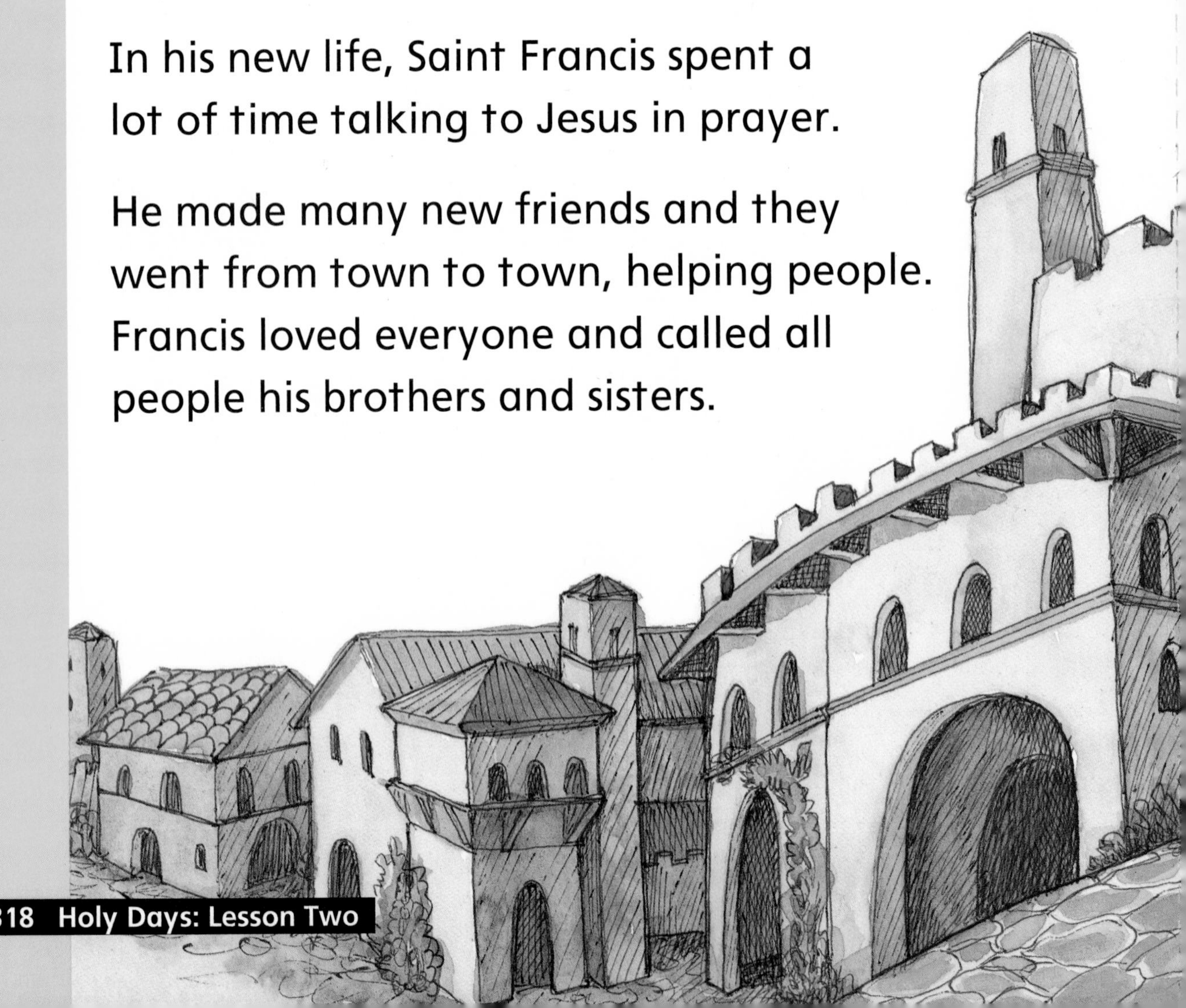

Francis made friends with the animals. He called them his brothers and sisters, too. Francis teaches us to care for everyone and everything that God makes.

We celebrate the feast of Saint Francis on October 4.

We pray, “Loving God, we praise and thank you for all your gifts.”

Activity

Name a person or thing you can show care for.

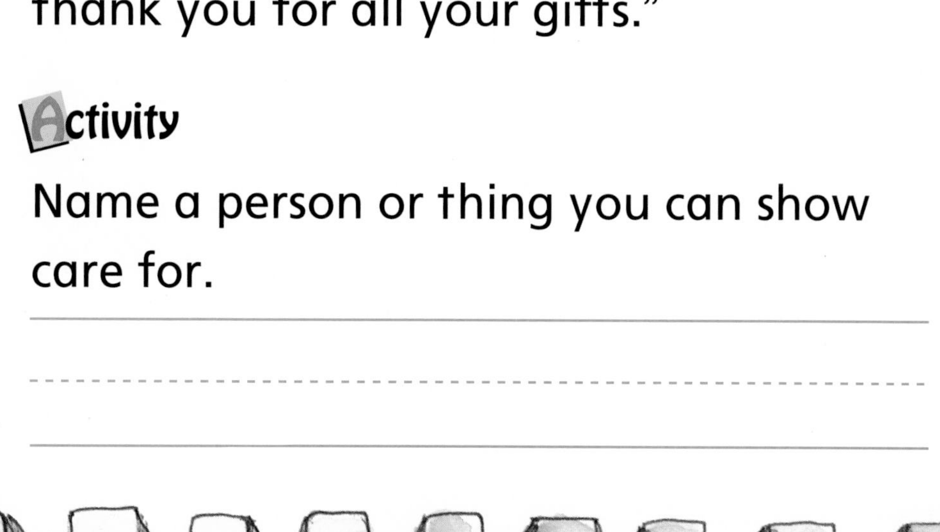

Sunday

Sunday is a holy day.
On Sunday, Catholics go to Mass.
We celebrate Jesus' new life at Mass.
Jesus shares a special meal with us.

On Sunday, God wants us to share
happy times with our families.
We can have a picnic, play games,
or visit new places.
We can have fun together.

Sunday is a special day because
it is God's day.

Activity

Look at what families can do on Sunday.
In each picture there is a hidden letter.
Find the letters and write them in the boxes.

What word do the letters make?

Add the word to the sentence below.

Sunday is ______________________.

In the Spirit of Jesus

Helen Keller

Helen Keller could not see,
hear, or talk.
But one day a teacher, Anne
Sullivan, came to help Helen.
Anne taught Helen to use
her hands to sign.

When Helen grew up, she
helped children who could not
see or hear or talk.
She started special schools
for them.

We can be like Helen Keller.
We can help others.

We pray,
"God, let us help others."

Activity

Learn the actions for the prayer.
Look at the pictures to help you.
Trace the letters for some of
the words.

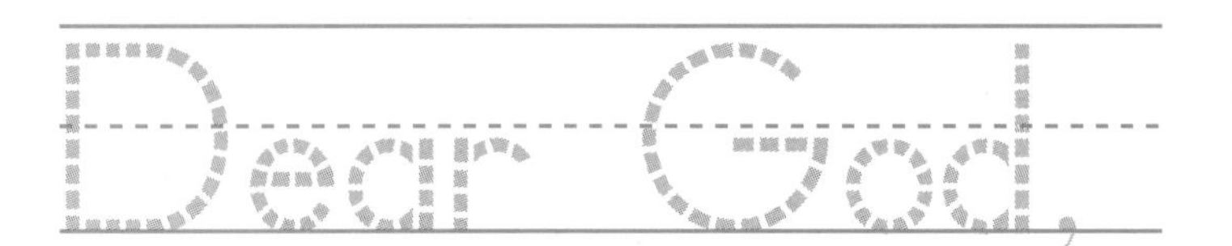

Help us always to trust you.

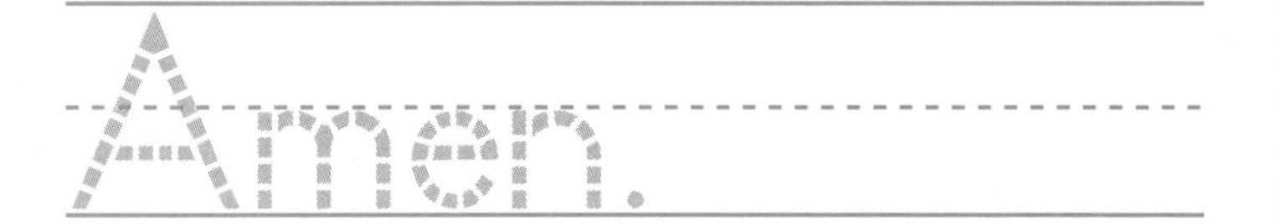

The Food Pantry

Sister Jean's class visited St. Mark
Food Pantry.
Sister Jean said, "Some families have
no money for food.
They can get food here."

The pantry was almost empty.
Sister Jean said, "The pantry needs food.
Would you like to help feed hungry families?"

"Yes!" said the boys and girls.

The children asked their parents what food
they could bring from home.
They put the food on the pantry shelves.
Sister Jean said, "Thank you for sharing.
I can see that you are trying to be like Jesus."

What kind of food could you bring to your parish food pantry? Draw some of your favorite foods on the pantry shelves.

Trace the word in the prayer below. Then say the prayer together.

Dear Jesus, help us to be like you.

Help us to share with others.

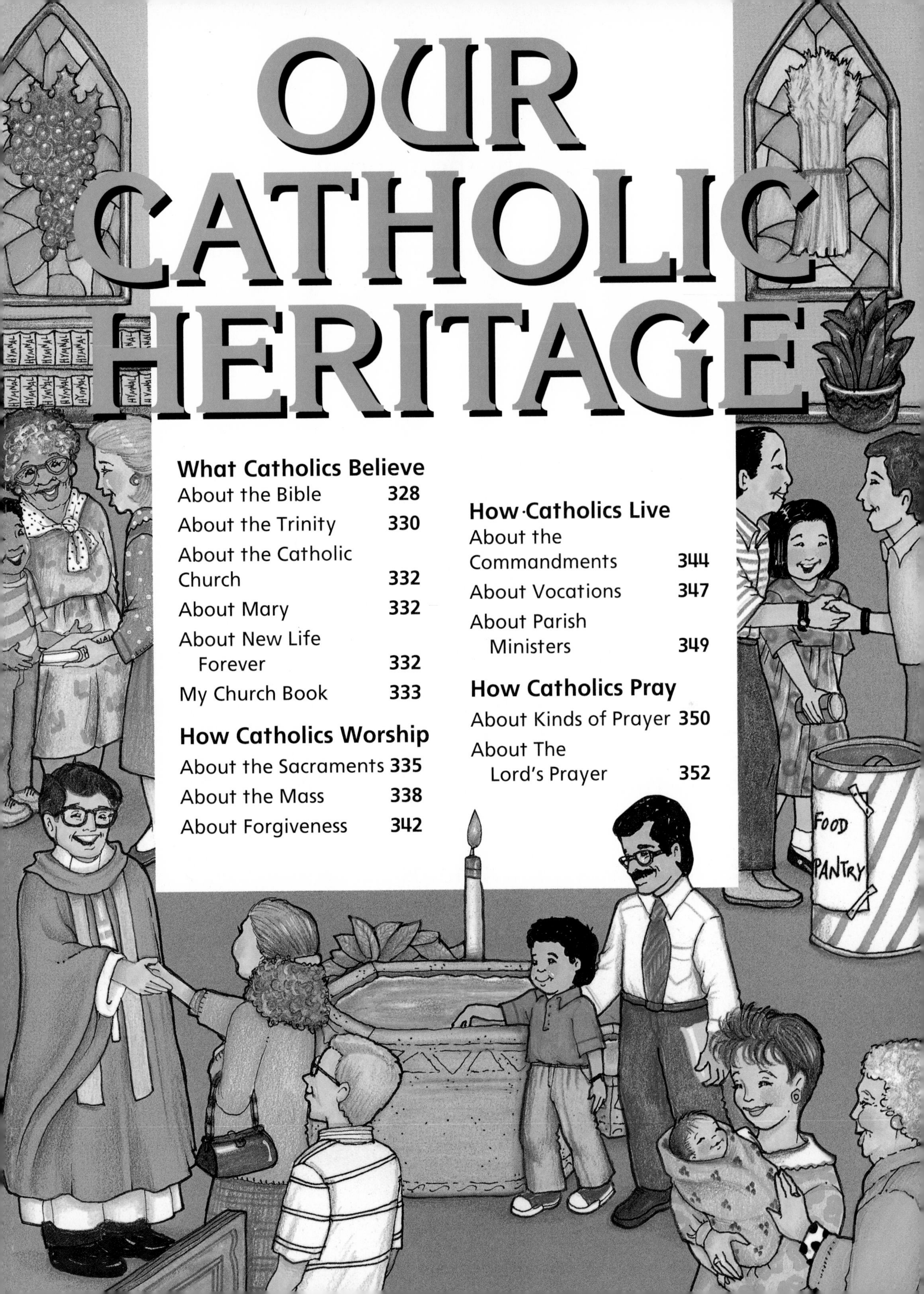

OUR CATHOLIC HERITAGE

What Catholics Believe

How Catholics Worship

How Catholics Live

How Catholics Pray

What Catholics Believe

Catholic Christians share many
special gifts.
We believe, live, and pray as one family.

ABOUT the Bible

The Bible is a special book
about God's love for us.
The Bible has many books.
Each book was written by someone
specially chosen by God.

We can read about God's love
for us in the Bible.
We can read about Jesus
and his followers.
We can also read about
how the Holy Spirit helps us.

In the Bible are stories of
Jesus and his followers.
The stories tell about
the things Jesus said and did.
They tell of the places where Jesus lived and visited.
The map on the next page shows some of the places.

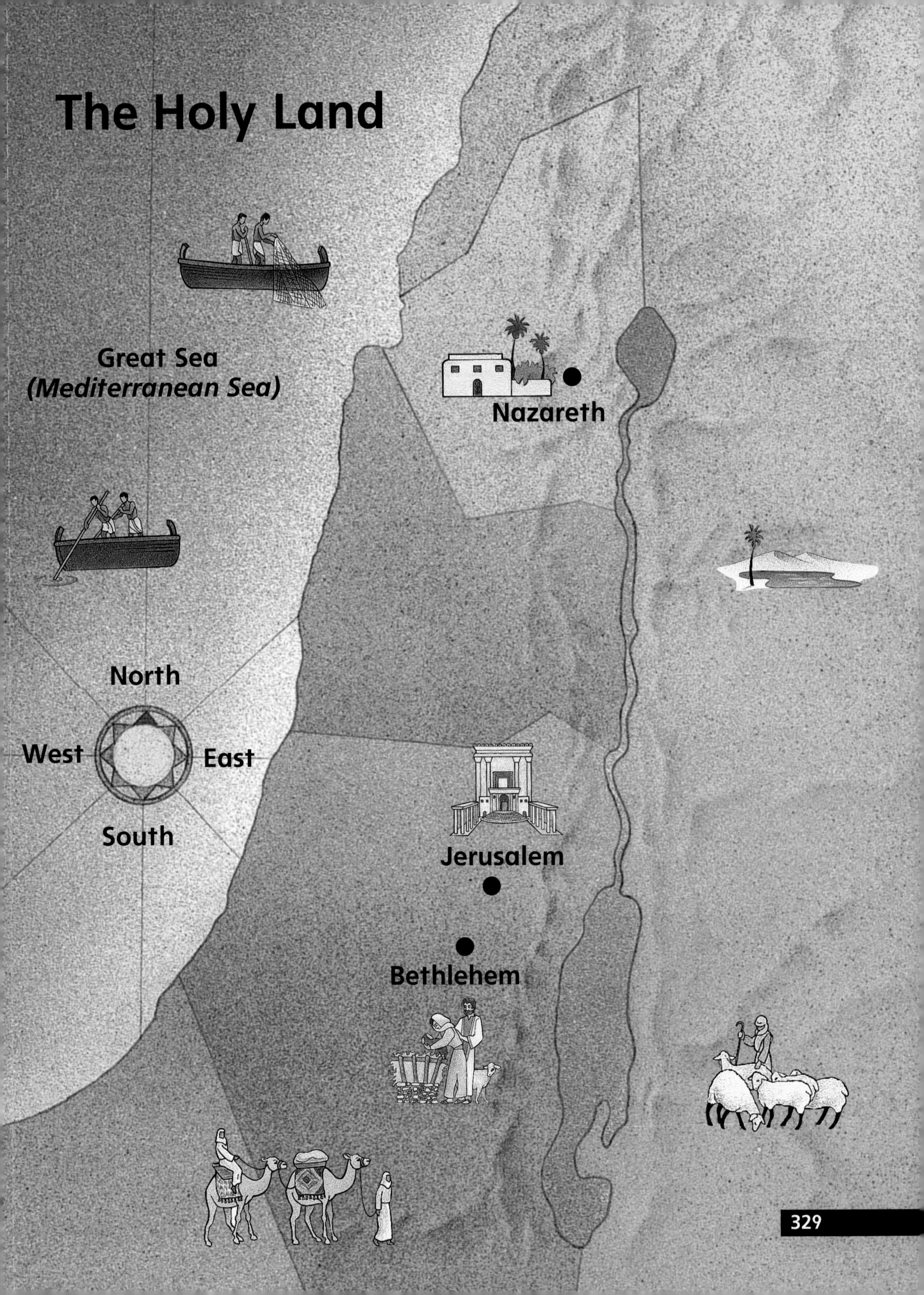
The Holy Land
Great Sea
(Mediterranean Sea)
Nazareth
North
West
East
South
Jerusalem
Bethlehem

ABOUT the Trinity

There is one God.
God is three persons—Father, Son, and Holy Spirit.

We Believe in God

God is our Creator.
God made all things with love.
Everything God made is good.

God speaks to us in the Bible, a special book about God's love.

God loves and cares for us.
God wants us to be happy.
God, our Father, sent us Jesus to help us.

We Believe in Jesus

Jesus is the Son of God.
God the Son became a man.
Jesus is our brother and friend.
He is one of us.

Jesus is our teacher.
Jesus teaches us about God.
God sent Jesus to show us how to love.

Jesus died on the cross and rose
from the dead for us.
Jesus is our **Savior**.
He saves us from sin and death.

Jesus is alive.
He shares new life with us.

We Believe in the Holy Spirit

The Holy Spirit is God.
The Holy Spirit is with us.
The Holy Spirit helps us follow Jesus.
The Holy Spirit gives us gifts to help
us live good lives.

ABOUT the Catholic Church

We are **Catholic Christians**.
Catholics celebrate the **sacraments**.
We pray to God and help others.

The pope is the leader of the
Catholic Church.
We call the pope our Holy Father.

The Church is the family of Jesus.
We tell the good news about Jesus.

ABOUT Mary

God chose Mary to be Jesus' mother.
Mary loved and trusted God.
Mary is our Mother, too.
Mary loves and cares for us.

ABOUT New Life Forever

Jesus teaches us that if we act with love,
we will be happy with God in **heaven**.
Heaven is being happy with God forever.

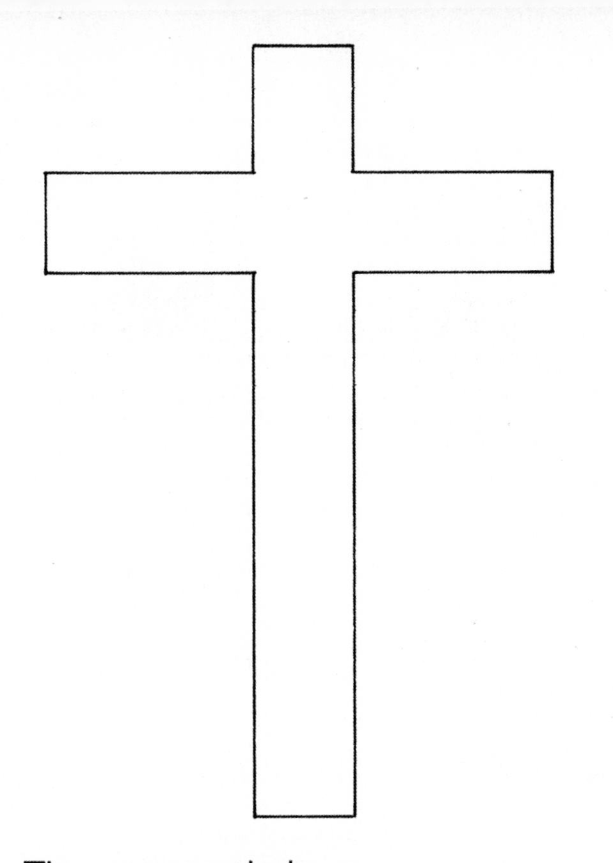

The cross reminds us
of Jesus, our friend and brother.

6

I belong to the
Catholic church.

3

fold

This statue reminds us
of Mary, the mother of Jesus.

8

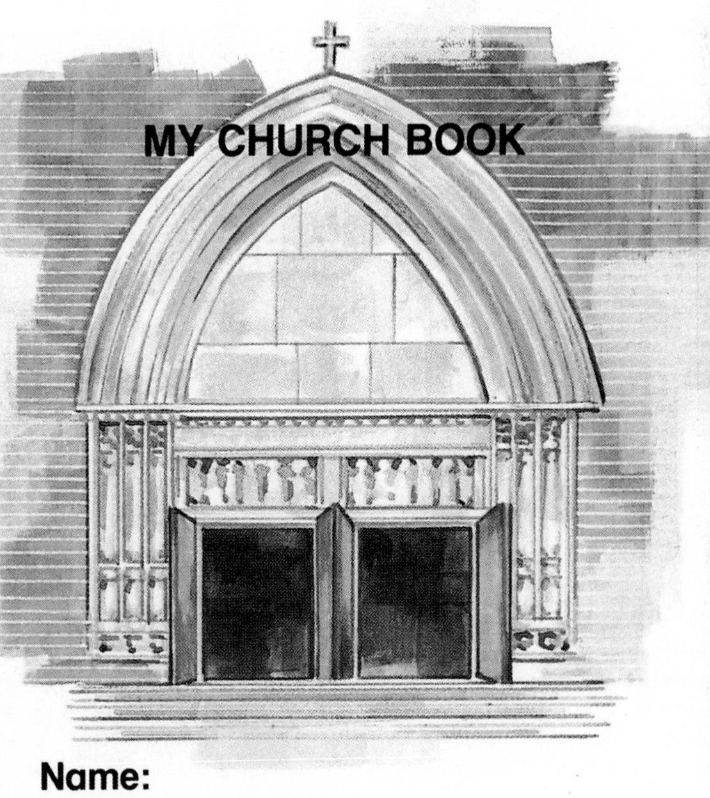

Name:

1

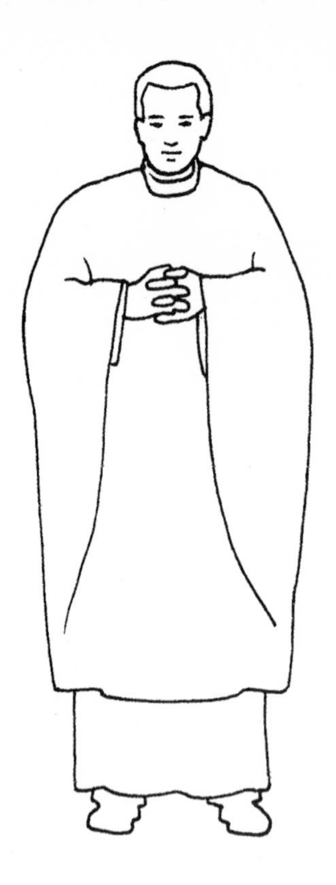

The priest is the parish leader.

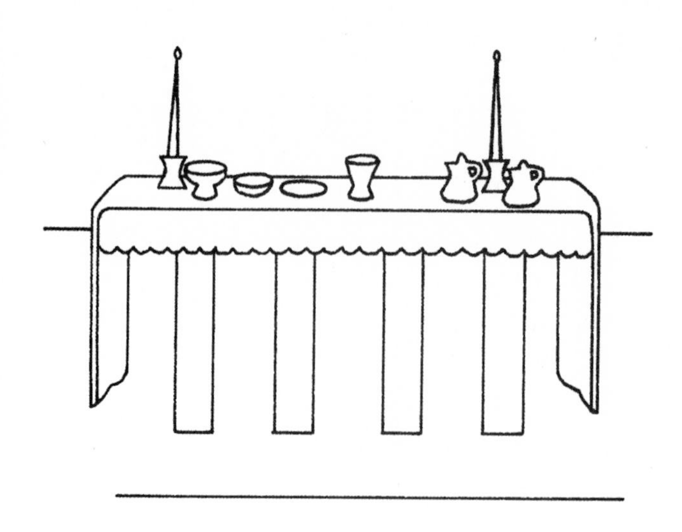

The altar reminds us
of our special
meal with Jesus.

The name of our parish church is

The lectern reminds us
that God, our Father,
and Jesus speak to us.

How Catholics Worship

Worship is giving honor and praise to God.
We worship God in prayer and
the sacraments.

ABOUT the Sacraments

The **seven sacraments** are celebrations
of God's love and Jesus' presence.

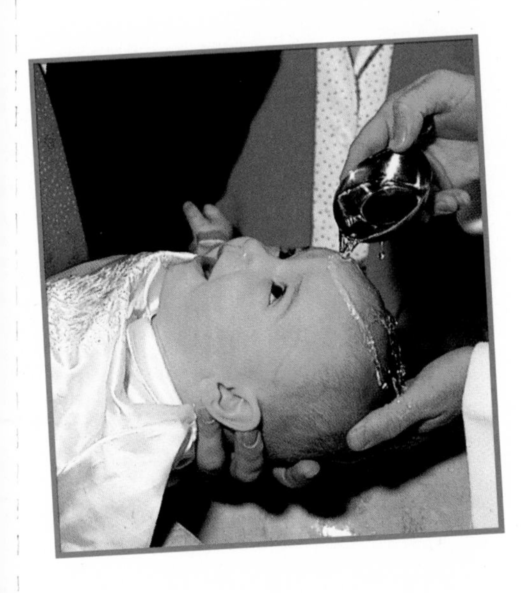

Baptism is a sacrament of
welcome into the Church.
At Baptism we receive
the Holy Spirit.
We are baptized with water.
The water is a sign that we
share Jesus' new life.

At **Confirmation**, we
receive the Holy Spirit
in a new way.
The Holy Spirit helps
us tell everyone about
Jesus' good news.

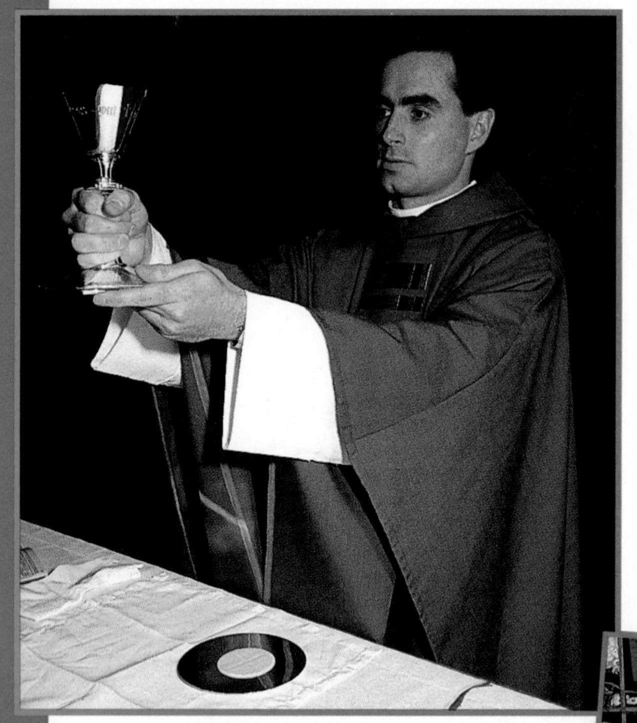

We celebrate the **Eucharist,** or the Mass, when we share a special meal with Jesus. In the Eucharist, Jesus gives himself to us as the Bread of Life.

In the Sacrament of **Reconciliation,** we say we are sorry for our sins.

The **Anointing of the Sick** brings Jesus' peace and help to sick people.

In the sacrament of **Holy Orders,** men become priests and join in Jesus' work in a special way.

The sacrament of **Marriage** celebrates the love of a man and a woman for each other.

ABOUT the Mass

1. Our celebration begins.
   The priest and other ministers
   walk down the aisle in
   a procession.
   We stand to sing a song.

2. To welcome us the priest says,
   "The Lord be with you."
   We answer, "And also
   with you."
   We all make the Sign of
   the Cross.

3. We remember our sins and
   God's love and forgiveness.
   The priest prays an
   opening prayer.

4. We listen to God's word
   in readings from
   the Old Testament and
   the New Testament.

5. In the gospel story, we hear about Jesus' life and teachings.
   We stand to welcome Jesus in the gospel.

6. The priest or deacon explains the readings to us in a special talk called a homily.

7. We pray for the Church, for our country, and for all God's people.
   We call this prayer the Prayer of the Faithful.

8. We bring gifts to prepare the altar for the meal.
   The gifts are the bread and wine.
   We always bring ourselves, our most important gift.

9. The priest offers our gift of bread to God.
The priest offers our gift of wine to God.

10. We thank and praise God for all God's blessings, especially for the gift of Jesus.

11. Our gifts of bread and wine become for us the body and blood of Jesus.

12. The priest holds up the body and blood of Jesus. He prays a prayer of praise.
We answer, "Amen!"

13. We pray together the prayer that Jesus taught us, The Lord's Prayer.

14. We offer one another a sign of peace to show that we are all brothers and sisters in Jesus.

15. We come to the table of the Lord to receive Jesus in the Eucharist.

16. We receive God's blessing and answer, "Amen."
We sing a song of praise.
Then we go in peace to love and serve all people.

ABOUT Forgiveness

Jesus loves me.
Jesus teaches me to
care for others.

When I do not love others
as I should, Jesus forgives me.

When I do not always do what he
wants me to do, Jesus forgives me.

I can pray,

"Jesus, I trust in your love.

I am sorry for all the wrong things I have done.

I am sorry for all the good things I have not done.

Jesus, I want to love you with all my heart."

How Catholics Live

Jesus teaches us how to live.
He gives us the Holy Spirit and the
Church to help us.

The Great Commandment

Jesus said, “You must love God above all things and love your neighbor as yourself” (Based on Mark 12:30-31).

Jesus’ **Great Commandment** tells us to show love for God and for our neighbor.

ABOUT the Commandments

We Live God’s Laws	
We show our love for God.	We believe in God and love God. We use God’s name with love. We pray to God every day. We pray with our Church family at Mass.
We show love for our neighbor.	We obey our parents and those who care for us. We care for all living things. We tell the truth. We are careful with other people’s things. We share with others and are thankful for God’s gifts.

Jesus' New Commandment

Jesus gave us a new commandment. He said, "Love one another as I love you" (Based on John 15:12).

We can love as Jesus loves by being fair and kind to all people.
We can help others.
We can be forgiving.

When we do not act with love, we **sin**.
Sin is choosing to do something we know is wrong.

The Holy Spirit Helps Us

We can choose to love or to sin.
The Holy Spirit helps us choose to love.

ABOUT Vocations

When we were baptized, we began
our new life as Catholic Christians.
God calls each of us to help others
in a special way.
This is called our **vocation**.

Many Ways of Helping

Here are some ways Catholics can
help others.

They can help at Mass by reading,
leading the songs, or giving the Bread
of Life to people.

They can teach about God and Jesus'
message in the gospels.

They can do other things to help too.

Sometimes God calls people to a special way of helping in the Church.
There are priests who lead the parish community.

There are religious brothers and sisters who teach, serve the poor, or help lead the parish.

There are deacons who pray with us and help us to care for those in need.

As you get older, you will discover in what special ways God is calling you to be a helper.

People Who Serve the Church

We belong to our parish Church.
At church and school, we see many people who serve the friends of Jesus.

The priest is the leader of the parish Church.
He celebrates the Mass and the sacraments with the people.
He cares for God's people.

At Mass, we might also see religious sisters, brothers, and deacons.
They help with the Sunday celebration.

They might also be teachers in the school.
They also lead the friends of Jesus in caring for others.

God invites all Catholics to take part in helping others through their parish Church.

How Catholics Pray

Prayer is talking and listening to God. God always hears our prayers.

We can pray alone or with others.

The Mass is our greatest prayer.

ABOUT Kinds of Prayer

We can praise God for our wonderful world.

We can thank God for the gift of our families and friends.

We can ask God to help us live as Jesus taught us.

We can say, "I love you, God."

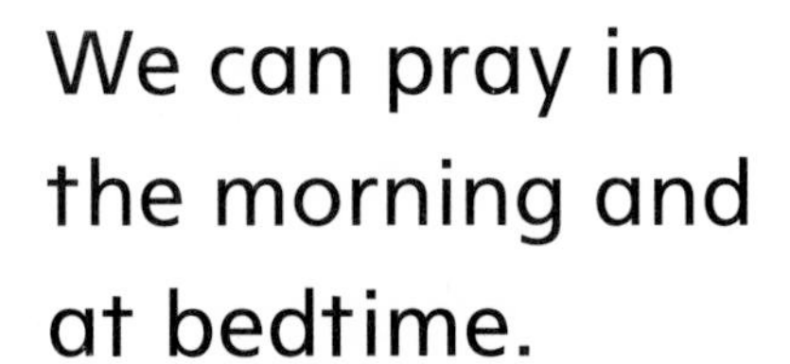

We can pray in the morning and at bedtime.

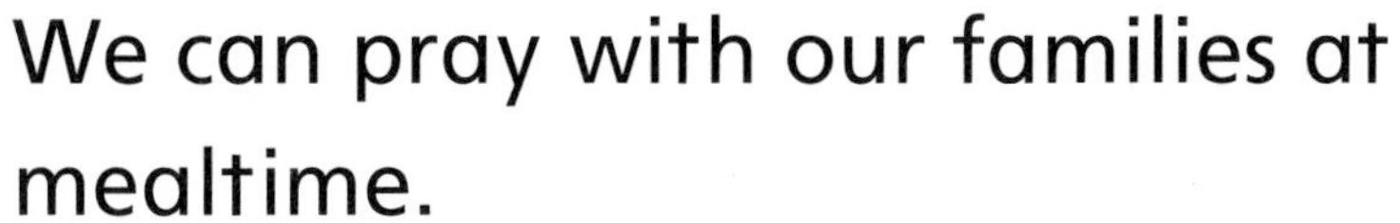

We can pray with our families at mealtime.

We can pray in school with our teacher and classmates.

At Sunday Mass, we pray with our families and the whole family of Jesus' friends.

ABOUT The Lord's Prayer

Jesus taught his friends **The Lord's Prayer**.
In this special prayer, we honor God.
We ask God for the things we need.

Our Father, who art in heaven, hallowed be thy name.

God is our Father.
We pray that everyone will remember how good God is.

Thy kingdom come;

Jesus told us about God's kingdom.
We pray that everyone will live as Jesus taught us to live.

thy will be done on earth as it is in heaven.

We pray that everyone will obey God's laws.

Give us this day our daily bread;

Our good God cares for us.
We pray for our needs and the needs of the poor.

and forgive us our trespasses as we forgive those who trespass against us;

We ask God to forgive us for the wrong things we have done.

and lead us not into temptation,

We ask God to help us always to choose what is right.

but deliver us from evil.

We pray that God will protect us from things that may harm us.

Amen.

Our "Amen" says that Jesus' prayer is our prayer, too.

WRITE-IN GLOSSARY

Advent

______________________ is four weeks of preparing for Christmas.

angel

An ______________________ is a messenger and helper from God.

Anointing of the Sick

______________________ is a sacrament that brings Jesus' peace and help to sick people.

Ash Wednesday

______________________ is the day the priest marks our foreheads with ashes. It is the first day of Lent.

Holy Orders ______________________ is the sacrament in which men become priests.

Baptism ______________________ is a celebration of our new life with Jesus and his friends.

Bible The ______________________ is a special book about God's love for us.

Christ The name ______________________ means that "Jesus was sent by God to help all people."

Christian A ______________________ is a friend and follower of Christ.

Church We belong to the Catholic ______________________
The word church also means a special place where Christians come together to pray.

Confirmation ______________________
is the sacrament in which we receive the Holy Spirit in a special way.

Create ______________________
means to make something out of nothing.

Creator Our ______________________ is God,
who makes everything in the world out of nothing.

Easter ______________________
is the celebration of Jesus being raised from the dead.

Emmanuel ______________________
means God is with us.

Epiphany On ______________________
we celebrate the feast of the wise men who followed the star to find Jesus.

Eucharist The ______ is the sacrament that celebrates Jesus' special meal.

Forgive ______ means to excuse or to pardon.

Galilee ______ is the area where Jesus grew up.

Godparents ______ are the people who help us grow as friends and followers of Jesus.

Good Friday ______ is the day we celebrate Jesus' death on the cross.

Good Samaritan The ______ was a person who cared for someone who needed help.

gospel The ______________________ is the good news of Jesus found in the Bible.

Great Commandment The ______________________ ______________________ tells us how to show love for God and our neighbor.

Hallowed ______________________ means holy.

Heaven ______________________ is being happy with God forever.

Holy Family Mary, Joseph, and Jesus are the ______________________.

Holy Saturday ______________________ night we begin our Easter celebration.

Holy Spirit The ______________________ is the Spirit of God.

Holy Thursday ______________________ is the day we celebrate the special meal when Jesus gave us his body and blood to share.

Jesus ______________________ is God's Son and our friend.

Joseph ______________________ is the husband of Mary who helped her raise Jesus.

Lent ______________________ is the forty days we prepare before Easter.

Marriage The sacrament of ______________________ celebrates the love of a man and woman.

Mary ______________________ is the mother of Jesus and our Mother, too.

Mass The ______________________ is a special meal Jesus shares with us.

Nazareth ______________________ is the town where Jesus lived with Mary and Joseph.

Passion Sunday ______________________ is the first day of Holy Week.

Peter and Andrew ______________________ were brothers. They were good friends of Jesus.

Prayer	________ is listening and talking to God.
rabbi	When Jesus was a boy a ________ was someone who taught about God and about life.
Reconciliation	The sacrament of ________ celebrates God's forgiveness.
sacrament	A ________ is a celebration of Jesus' love and God's presence.
saint	A ________ is someone who loves Jesus and others very much. He or she is a very special follower of Jesus.
Savior	Our ________ is Jesus, the Son of God and our friend. He saves us and helps us.

Sin ______________________ is choosing to do something we know is wrong.

Sunday ______________________ is a holy day when we celebrate Jesus' rising from the dead.

Temple The ______________________ was a holy place in the city of Jerusalem where people prayed and learned about God.

Trespass ______________________ means to hurt someone.

Trust ______________________ means to believe in someone's love for us.

Worship ______________________ means to give honor and praise to God.